Identity as Strategy

For Bram and Guus.

BIS Publishers
Timorplein 46
1094 CC Amsterdam
The Netherlands
bis@bispublishers.com
www.bispublishers.com

ISBN 978 90 636 9879 9

Identity as Strategy

How your
corporate identity
can fuel your success

Stijn van Diemen

BIS Publishers

Contents.

Preface.

Nada nos maravilla tanto como el descubrimiento de lo que ya sabíamos.

Antonio Muñoz Molina.

The concept of identity has been my faithful companion for some thirty years now. Whether from a purely design-led perspective, or in corporate identity and branding projects and programmes, or in the positioning and marketing of organisations, sectors and territories, or in the development of organisational strategies, identity has always been connecting the dots. It has played its part as the visual and communicative centre of branding, as the key connective element in marketing, and as the guiding principle and starting point for strategies. I have learnt that it can tell compelling stories, guide daily work, pave the way for development, innovate organisations, create regional coherence, forge surprising but valuable connections, ... And all the while, and in all the challenges I have been asked to help with, I have become more and more fascinated by its nature. What is identity if it can do all this? How can something so intangible be as strong as I experienced it to be? How is it possible that we can share an understanding of something that no one really knows how to describe? Why do we trust it so much? And why does it seem so constant and untouchable?

One of the nice things about identity is that everything and everyone has one. It's just there, whether you know it or like it or not. Being aware of who you are would seem to be a natural thing, but in my experience it is not. We take our identity for granted. It's inescapable us and ours alone. And that's what's fascinating about it — for me, anyway. That no matter what happens to you, and no matter how it changes you, you will still be you. Now why is that?
I firmly believe that the answer lies in the values that make up any identity. Becoming someone or something, developing and

displaying a personality, defining the relationship between you and the world you live or operate in — all depend on the values you hold. I have learnt that staying true to yourself, to your values, is the best guarantee of success for any organisation, sector or region. More than that, I believe that by staying true to your values, you actually become yourself and build a stronger personality every time you make a choice. You do not freely 'choose' and activate an identity — because that would mean that you are not being true to yourself, but to external goals. Sooner or later you will either lose track of yourself, or the environment will 'unmask' you. But if you consistently reflect on the meaning of your values, you will always be yourself.

In this sense, there is an ethical dimension to identity, or more precisely, ethics is part of identity. Living up to yourself means living up to your values. If you do not make yourself a steward of what you hold dear, you are ignoring who you are. And since no organisation, region or sector lives in splendid isolation, this means that your identity is also part of the public debate about the quality and development of your context. In other words, being who you are means playing a role in the world around you.

We live in an extremely interconnected world. It may not, as is often said, be getting more complex per se, but we are now extremely connected, we know about more coexisting complexities and, to make matters worse, we know about the connections between those complexities. As complexity increases, we ourselves need to be consistent to deal with it. We need conduct principles rather than targets. Conduct principles, based on values. That is, identities. As I have said, if you live by goals with an 'external' definition, you will be volatile. This belief has been a steady drumbeat throughout my career: that in order to have real meaning and responsibility, you need to show and live up to your values. And that you can do this through conduct that is your own, that affirms you, that is simply 'the way you do things', recognisable and understandable.

I have learned to trust the relationship between consistency and complexity by looking at this relationship from an identity perspective. Grounding what you do in your identity will enable you to make the right strategic decisions (even under pressure) because you will be guided not only by what you have to do, but also by what you want. Who do you want to be, what kind of country do you want to live in, what kind of organisation do you want to work for, which organisations and people people do you want to work with? Following your own ambitions and values, while facing your challenges, will make you a continuous and responsible factor in any changing environment — and therefore a strong player. I learned that this, and much more, is what identity can do. And I would like to share my discoveries with you, hoping to fuel your success.

ntroduction

What identity can do for your strategy.

Suppose you are someone who works on the management of an organisation, its strategy, marketing or CSR. Or your job is to position, protect or develop a region. Or you have some responsibility for a sector and need to be able to identify and respond to the challenges facing that sector. You might be a manager, civil servant, politician, project developer, consultant or expert. In these roles, you will have to make or support strategic decisions from time to time. And in doing so, you will have experienced the dilemma between evolution and consistency. Between complexity and clarity. Between change and continuity. How do you ensure that your strategic decisions take you to the next level, but are also understandable, logical and feasible?

This book will help you resolve these dilemmas and make these choices by bringing the identity of your organisation, region or sector into play. I describe examples, models and programmes that will show you what awareness of your identity can do for you and help you harness the power of that identity. The book will tell you how to stay true to yourself while charting a clear course for your development. How to make choices that reflect your loyalty to who you are while responding to the challenges you face. How your purpose and responsibilities define you. It will tell you about the relationship between values and identity, and the perspectives that your identity can give you on your choices, ambitions, developments and relationships. In short, it will tell you what being aware of your identity can do for your strategy.

Firstly because, as I said, it will enable you to make better strategic decisions. If you base yourself on consistent beliefs, which you will naturally do if you are aware of who you are and what that means, you will have clarity about where you want to go. 'We've come from here, we've experienced all this, we've learned all this, so the next logical step is this. Not because "we always do it this way", but because we know who we are, what we want to achieve, what our role is and where we can go. Because we can envision a future based on our past. If we are aware of the values we hold and what they will mean in that future, we will always know what to do.'

Secondly, because it will enable you to build a better organisation, a more prosperous region, a more structured and effective sector. If you are aware of the identity of your organisation, region or sector and where you want to go, you will know how to organise yourself. 'What do we need to play our part, how do we balance our resources, efforts and challenges, how do we track our success, who do we work with?' The answers to these questions will not be easier (your identity is not a magic wand), but they will be more logical and explainable. 'This is how we do it — because this is who we are. We respond to challenges and expectations by being true to ourselves and our values.' No one will doubt you.

Another way in which this book can contribute to your succes is that it will help you stay on track, whatever happens. Everyone who has responsibility experiences difficult moments when everything seems to go wrong, when opponents seem to have everything right, when doubts grow about the course you have taken. In these moments it is extremely helpful and valuable to reflect on who you are, what has made you that, and what this means for you and your next steps. You'll see that you can follow a clear path, play a certain role, respond to competitors and opponents by being true to yourself and basing your response to changing contexts and new challenges on your identity.

This book will show you how to inspire those around you. By sharing who you are, the values you hold and the role you want to play, your peers, employees, partners and stakeholders will not only understand you better, they will experience leadership. They will recognise, acknowledge and learn from your values, ambitions and choices. Knowing who you are and acting on it will inspire many and strengthen the role you want to play.

A final topic that I address this book is how to overcome what I would like to call 'excessive brand focus'. You will find several places in this book where I describe the difference between 'identity' on the one hand and 'brand' on the other. I will comment on the value and strength of these concepts for your organisation, region or sector. Brands are psychological constructs in the minds of your target audiences, perceptions of your importance; they should not be confused with the personality and character that will ultimately lead you to make the right decisions in the long run. After all, it is you, not your audience, who should determine your strategy.

This book consists of seven chapters and an epilogue. Each describes a case study from my own experience, looks at the identity aspects of that case, and offers a specific perspective on what identity meant and did in that case — and can do in others. The book presents models that can be used, design principles that you can apply yourself, and definitions that might help you reflect on yourself. Rather than trying to be a showroom of cases, these cases are meant to be thought-provoking and offer ways of explaining what an identity perspective can mean for any organisation, sector or region — including yours.

I will start out by describing some basic dimensions of identity. How does the concept of identity relate to concepts such as 'ambition', 'interaction', 'origin', 'drive and energy', 'inside and outside'? Please bear with me through this somewhat abstract first chapter, as we will need these 'academic' definitions for the more practical applications I will describe in the rest of the book.

Next, I focus on the guiding principles that your identity provides; in other words, the logic that is a natural part of who you are. If you can define what you actually do and make that manifest in a way that is understandable and inspiring to you and those around you, you will demonstrate your value and relevance.

In the third chapter I will talk about the relationship between identity and strategy, mainly from the perspective of your ambitions and how you can work on those ambitions, and in Chapter 4 I will present identity as a collective development dimension and a basis for innovative capacity. Moreover, I will talk about the ethical aspects of identity.

Chapter 5 is dedicated to collaboration and partnership. It describes how identity serves as a recognisable touchpoint for the environment and creates opportunities for collaboration. Stakeholder management is the central theme of the sixth chapter: Identity can act as a 'sensing model' for your position and connection with your environment. Chapter 7 looks at project, programme and process management. Here, identity is presented as a reference point in time, in spatial aspects, in stakeholder environments and in environmental dynamics.

Finally, I wrap things up with an epilogue which deals with aspects of the process of self-reflection. This epilogue is more process-oriented and less about the relevance of identity as such; at the same time it shows how identity serves as a link and inspiration for the daily life in the office and the reasons why we come to this office every day.

So, in retrospect, here's a quick summary of what identity can do for your strategy: it can define you, guide you, share and justify your ambitions, connect you, support change, make you relevant and keep everyone involved. But most of all, it can inspire you to be your best self, simply by virtue of its intriguing nature as an important yet intangible asset of your organisation, region or sector.
With this book, I hope to share with you some of my fascination with the enigmatic, dynamic and multifaceted nature of identity, and inspire you to think about what it can do for you.

Before diving into the cases and chapters, a brief word about what I call 'A Designer's Fate'. If you would look at the current state of things of the cases I describe in this book, especially the older ones, you will see that in the real world things are not (quite) as I describe them here. Names and brands may have changed, organisations may have disappeared or merged, sectors may have been reorganised. This is the life of a creative consultant or designer: over time, clients take the next step, possibly with other consultants and designers, and change or even discard the results of the previous collaboration. Or so it might seem. All development of organisations, sectors or regions is made up of steps and phases, showing a growing insight and awareness of who one is. New challenges require new answers — and I believe that these answers can be consistent if one is sufficiently aware of one's identity and values. In other words, there is no fundamental break in development, and the steps taken after we have left as consultants or designers are only possible because of the steps we have taken together. A designer's fate, then, is to accept the ephemeral nature of his work: precisely because it is effective, it will be superseded by the client.
We accept our fate with resignation.

Identity, interaction and
consistency.

Basic definitions.

Floriade World Expo 2022
'Holland Central' reveals
the value of a region.

Corporate identity and
corporate image.

1

Identity and alterity.

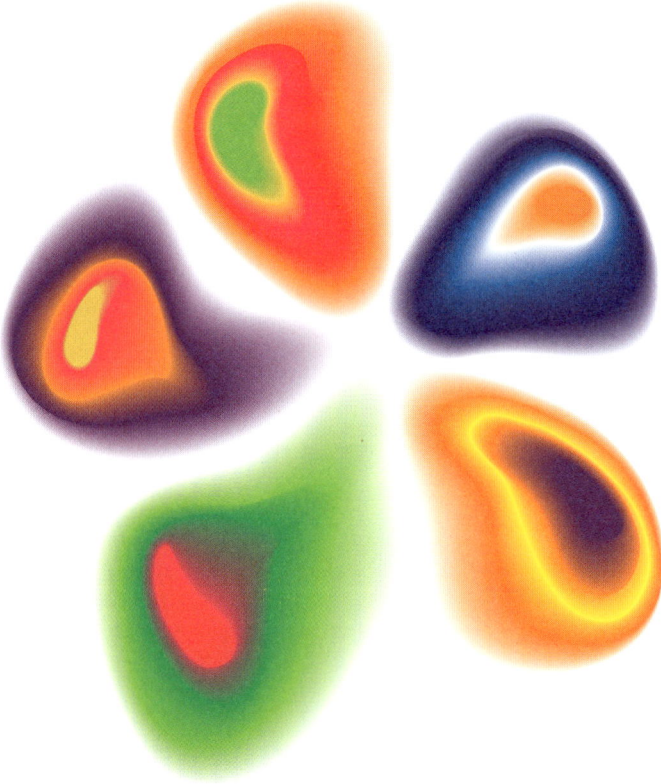

WORLD EXPO
HOLLAND CENTRAL
FLORIADE 2022

Floriade World Expo 2022.
How a region discovered and activated its value.

The Floriade World Expo was an event that took place in the Netherlands every 10 years between 1960 and 2022.[1] It showcased and discussed the latest developments in horticulture, a field in which the Netherlands is particularly strong. It was organised by the Dutch National Horticultural Council (Nationale Tuinbouwraad or NTR) and targeted the international community of growers and traders of food, flowers and plants, as well as the general public. The event typically attracted between two and three million visitors.

Floriade had no proper facilities; in fact, it had no home base. Similar to the Olympic Games, the right to organise an edition of the Expo had to be won by bidding. So every 10 years a new bidding process was launched, with a general call for ideas to be expressed in a preliminary bid. The NTR then selected three or four candidate cities, which were allowed to develop their plans in a more detailed bid book.

In 2011, just before the start of Floriade 2012 (which took place in Venlo, in the south of the Netherlands), a new round of bidding was launched. As horticulture is an important economic sector in the Netherlands and Floriade is a very interesting opportunity for urban and cultural development (just like the Olympic Games), there was a lot of interest. Of the seven candidates in the first round, four were asked to prepare a bid book: the cities of Almere, Amsterdam and Groningen and the region of Boskoop. At the end of Floriade 2012, the NTR announced that the organisation of Floriade 2022 had been awarded to the city of Almere.

While working at Total Identity, I was part of the team that developed the bid book for the region of Boskoop (which ended in a glorious, but insufficient — and of course undeserved — second place). The team consisted of the region's municipalities, construction, consultancy and engineering companies, a healthcare organisation, the Chamber of Commerce, the

Note 1.
I speak in past tense here because after the 2022 edition of Floriade, the organisers realised that its concept had become more or less obsolete, and decided to end its existence in favour of other marketing and exhibiting channels.

Province of Zuid-Holland and the architecture firm OMA. We developed the vision, concept and implementation plan, the urban design approach and the marketing plan for Floriade in the 'Green Heart' of Holland, which was presented by the municipality of Boskoop as the representative. As always, my efforts were focused on the development of the vision, concept and strategy.

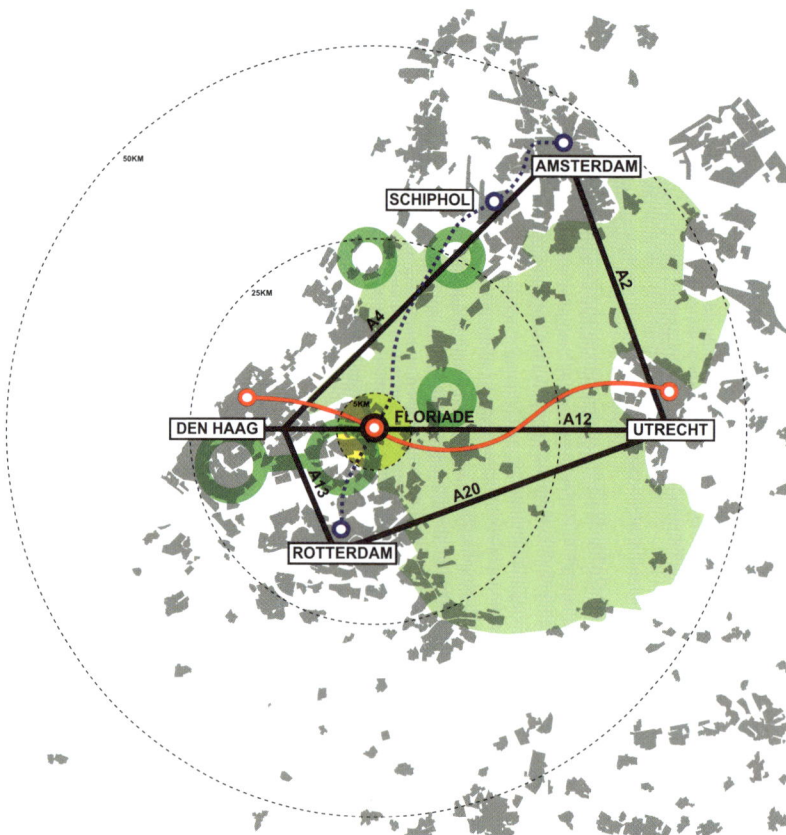

Figure 1.
The 'Randstad' and the proposed location of Floriade in the Boskoop-region.

Vision and concept

In the centre of the Netherlands lies the so-called 'Randstad', which consists of four major cities (Amsterdam, Utrecht, Rotterdam and The Hague) and the smaller towns and municipalities in between. Together they form a circular ('rand') conurbation ('stad') with a population of around eight million. The Randstad spans four provinces, contains two airports, Europe's largest seaport, industrial and employment areas, almost half of the Netherlands' universities, and important infrastructure and water areas.Surprisingly, most of the Randstad is agricultural land. In particular, the area within the 'circle' between the cities, the so-called 'Groene Hart' (Green Heart), consists of large, continuous agricultural and horticultural areas. This aspect makes the region of Boskoop, which lies in the Groene Hart between Rotterdam and The Hague and is one of the seven so-called 'Green Ports' that we have in the Netherlands, very interesting. Here, over the centuries, people have managed to develop a region with a balanced mix of urban, rural and wet (or 'red', 'green' and 'blue') areas. Despite the pressures of housing and feeding so many people in such a small area, the quality of life is very high. This has been achieved through centuries of very careful town and country planning on the one hand, and continuous intensification of agriculture and horticulture on the other.

FReflecvting on this character of the region, we came to a simple conclusion: Floriade is already here. You just don't see it. If Floriade is a showcase for what horticulture can achieve in terms of growing capacity, product quality, logistical efficiency and so on, then the Boskoop region is a living laboratory for all this. Inside the greenhouses, there is constant innovation in the cultivation of food, flowers and plants, both in terms of quantity and quality. The enormous quantity of produce compared to the relatively limited use of land and energy makes the production very sustainable. The logistics required to distribute the products (to the Randstad, national and international markets) are fully integrated into the area, both in terms of structure and working methods. And despite this productive capacity, the quality of housing, landscape and recreation is very high. This area has been a showcase for quality horticulture for centuries.

If this was true of the past, it should be true of the future. The organisation of a Floriade could be the driving force for the next development of the region, which should be in line with its history. So we wrote a 'region story' that did not end with the present but extended into the future. We chose the word 'vitality' as our leading concept: the vitality of the sector and of the area, of the economy, of the landscape, of the people who live and work here. Vitality appears here as the natural

Figure 2.
Proposition of the
GreenXChange.

successor to intensification that can guide us into the future. It can be a conduct principle for our future behaviour, always seeking solutions that bring new vitality.

In the history of the Netherlands, the relationship between products, trade and logistics has always been crucial. Our discovery in the seventeenth century, which brought us wealth and prosperity, was that in order to trade products you do not need to have them at hand. It is enough to know where they are and to provide the logistics from that point to the buyer. This idea made the Netherlands the world's first exchange. In other words, our knowledge of trade and logistics became perhaps even more important than production itself.

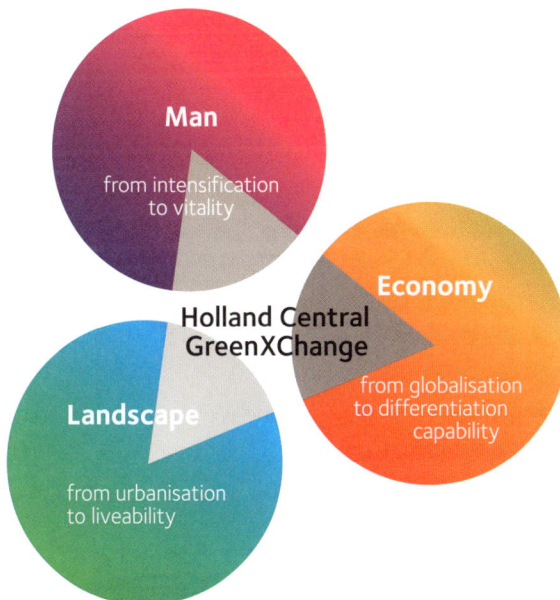

Figure 3.
Contextual significance of the GreenXChange.

The same could happen in the Boskoop region: the very specific knowledge of the trade and logistics of horticultural products that has been developed here could be translated into what we called 'GreenXChange': a central point for the trade and logistics of horticultural products, whether produced in the region or not. Such a GreenXChange would make the green sector more coherent, add value to make society more vital, strengthen cooperation between different economic players, facilitate the exchange of innovative ideas and products, and activate consumers towards a healthier and more vital lifestyle. Floriade should therefore be seen as the starting point for this Green XChange.

So the only thing to do was to make the hidden qualities of the region visible and accessible. We developed the idea of adding landmarks to the area to show its boundaries, content and coherence. OMA translated this idea into large objects to be placed in the landscape and gave these objects additional functionality to create entrances and connections to and within the area. We developed a marketing concept that used the 'Making of Floriade' as an central tool to show the world what's happening here and to attract the attention of professionals and the general public. And we focused specifically on Floriade's heritage, making our GreenXChange concept a possible reality.

Figure 4.
OMA's spatial
translation of
the concept for
Floriade 2022
in the Boskoop
region.

Identity aspects

Although Floriade was not awarded to the Boskoop region, there were some very interesting and valuable aspects to the effort: firstly, what is described here as a coherent region was not perceived as such when we started. It was only when we started to draw 'treasure maps' of the area, showing places of interest, landscape qualities, historical assets and infrastructure, and describing the possibilities in our conceptual approach, that the seven municipalities involved discovered what they had in common. It turned out that they were working together on the same thing, each contributing from their own perspective and interests. So the first legacy here was the common focus that was developed during the process.

The concept of vitality and the rationalisation of the development of the area in the 'GreenXChange' approach was the second important result. The value of what had been achieved in the region and the possibilities of extending this value into the future proved to be one of the most important outcomes of the project. The players in the region found themselves united in this single, unique conduct principle, 'vitality', which has driven and will continue to drive their economic and social success. With or without Floriade.

In both senses, we find identity to be a connective principle for this region. Not as a limitation or a law, but as an iteration between individual and shared values and aspects. Each company, organisation, community or inhabitant of this region is now more aware of the specific quality of the area and the contribution that can be made to this quality. In other words, the identity exists through the benefit of the counterparts: it is precisely because of the diversity of the region that it becomes coherent. It is a networked and fluid identity because all its components contribute their own value to it, bring about change by changing themselves, and in this sense are all important to the identity of the region as it emerges and develops.

So the story did not end when Floriade was not awarded. Not only did the people, companies and institutions of the region discover each other and their common character, but they also realised that, in order for this character to survive, they had a duty to extend it into the future. 'Now that we know who we are, we also know what and who depends on us,' as one of the mayors put it.

The identity of the region leads to a social commitment to continuity. Not in the sense of preservation, but in the sense of development. Its identity provides the region with a beacon in the surrounding dynamics and enables coherent transitions: this is where we come from, this is what we have done, this is where it has taken us — so something like GreenXChange could be our logical next step.

Identity and its meanings

We use the term 'identity' for many meanings. Identity can indicate individuality, recognisability, origin, continuity, will. Identity can be important, an incident, a benchmark, a coincidence, a burden. Moreover, what makes these meanings complex is that they can be perceived both internally and externally. 'Individuality' seems to indicate a personal aspect — but we recognise individuality by comparing with other identities. 'Descent' refers to both its owner and, by its nature, its predecessors. 'Will' is personal — but focuses on realisation in the external world.

Identity depends on relationship. The role of identity is largely external, without being consciously used in most cases: identity does not primarily want to distinguish, but it does. Every identity is shaped by and shapes the framework in which it forms the subject. Being a horticultural entrepreneur in the Boskoop region partly determines one's identity. At the same time, the Boskoop region is shaped by those who are part of it, whether as residents, politicians or entrepreneurs. So identity creates a framework, but also derives itself from it.

The different meaning of identity in its internal or external perception becomes fully visible when we realise that identity is born from our own individual will, from what drives us, unknowable and indefinable. Where the will is amorphous, an unguided projectile, identity is the perceptible form of it, the realisation of the will.

Identity gives us insight in the drive for self-realisation of its owner through the tension between the inside and the outside: whatever the individual wants, interacts with reality in the form of identity. In other words: identity is the manifestation of the will as it collides with external reality. It is the will of the individual in action, in communication.

Now if identity is formed in interaction with external reality, then that reality is, as it were, the completion of identity itself, and therefore co-determines it. Reality is a residual form, a mould for the will. Reality helps to shape what comes into contact with it. The collision of will with reality produces a perceptible identity that can only be understood in its context. In our "fluid times", as Baumann calls them, identity seems to have to be reinvented every day. (Or perhaps it's the other way round: in the transience of our modern context, identity offers a possible continuity. We'll return to this point in Chapter 4).

Identities express themselves in social behaviour. Behaviour is a reflection of the will, in bent, adapted form. The will that would want to realise itself directly is aggressive, unguided, and therefore ineffective. Behaviour as directly determined by the will is undesirable because, by its nature, it is not social and is therefore restricted in a social environment. This is how social manners and politics appear: the individual enters into negotiations with his environment to see that his interests are represented as much as possible. Social community can be seen as an extremely complex set of individual interests, weighed by all participants to serve their own interests. We give here and get there — the will compromises.

The form that the will takes in its appearance, the identity of the individual, in social context is often referred to as personality. 'Personalities colour our social existence,' we say. That positive opinion is interesting, since each personality actually results to be a disguised form of self-interest.

Identity and organisations

Organisations also have a will, which normally is referred to as 'ambition'. Whether we are talking about companies, public organisations, sectors, collaborations, regions, cities or countries: organisations mean business, and that word reflects will: the will to come to something: 'I do something because I want something, because I want to go somewhere.'

Organisations, just like persons, also have a context which is equally tinted by negotiation. The interests of organisations are pursued in a context in which competition, relevance, position and strategy are the leading concepts. But more than in the individual-social context, the drivers here are made public: organisational interests are shown more openly than personal interests.

And, finally, organisations have an identity, usually referred to as their corporate identity. Through this corporate identity (which is different from their 'brand', as I will discuss in Chapter 5), organisations give an insight into their will, their motivations, their ambitions. Identities are not primarily about differentiation, as is the case with brands, but about individuality and the right to exist.

I consider corporate identity to be one of the guiding principles of any organisation, region or sector. A corporate identity is based on shared values that in many cases led to the establishment or recognition as such, and precisely because of that permeates actions, gives direction to decisions, determines origin and future, and in the end creates recognition.

Corporate identity, the 'personality' of the organisation, cannot be read in itself and is necessarily expressed through channels such as appearance, messages or behaviour. More visibly than with individuals, the organisation deliberately creates an image of itself in reality. And more so than individuals, the organisation seeks to influence its own context. The external reality of the organisation therefore shows a coincidence of identity with the ambitions of the organisation. As mentioned above, organisational interests are easier to read than personal interests.

Identity and communications
We often and gladly use the famous Birkigt and Stadler model to describe identity and its channels. The model describes how the personality ('Selbstverständnis der Organisation, Wille') of the organisation expresses itself through conduct, communication and appearance and thus forms the externally

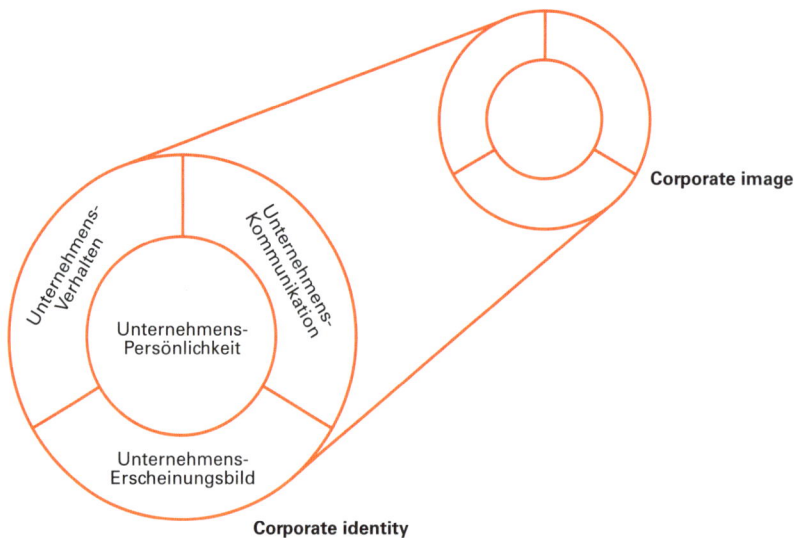

Corporate image

Unternehmens-Verhalten

Unternehmens-Kommunikation

Unternehmens-Persönlichkeit

Unternehmens-Erscheinungsbild

Corporate identity

Figure 5. Birkigt and Stadler's well-known representation of corporate identity.

perceptible corporate identity.[2] We define the actual perception of this constellation by the recipient as the image. And the model then states that that the image can be influenced by a conscious management of the corporate identity, with as its bearer the 'corporate story', the story of the organisation (see Chapter 4).

For me, two things stand out in the model: its one-sided orientation from inside to outside, and the absence of a description of the recipient of the image. But this is strange: in imagology, the science that studies the phenomenon of 'self-image', a distinction is made between 'identity' and 'alterity', i.e. one's own identity and the identity of the recipient. What is meant here is that the identity of the recipient of the image plays a major role in the actual perception. The knowledge, context and values of the 'other' also contribute to the image.

This makes every identity dependent on its perception, on its relationship to the alterities surrounding it. In other words, it makes identity relative. Here we encounter an interesting paradox: precisely because identities have to make themselves perceptible, they become part of an interaction that influences their perception.

If it is true that every identity is just as relative as all the others, then of course it becomes very difficult for any identity to distinguish itself, to convince of its relevance. After all, in principle any recipient can take the same position and claim that their perception is just as important as the intended message. A competing horticultural company from the south of Spain will have a very different perception of 'Boskoop' than a resident of the Boskoop region.
This has nothing to do with the actual identity of Boskoop, but rather with the shared or non-shared interests of the recipients: Boskoop entrepreneurs will all have roughly the same image of their Spanish colleagues because they have the same interests in that image.

Note 2.
The German word Verhalten is hard to translate. It means 'behaviour' as well as 'position in or relation to the environment'. There is an almost moral aspect to the word, an obligation towards the context. This is important, because often Verhalten is simply translated as 'behaviour', which does no right to the intention of the authors. For that reason, I prefer 'conduct'. The same goes for the word Erscheinungsbild, which in most cases is translated to 'symbols' which, in turn, sometimes even gets confused with the brand or the logotype. But it seems to me that Birkigt and Stadler have a much richer meaning in mind: the way the organisation deliberately appears in its totality.

Identity   Alterity

Alterity 2   Alterity 2

Identity   Alterity 1   Identity   Alterity 1

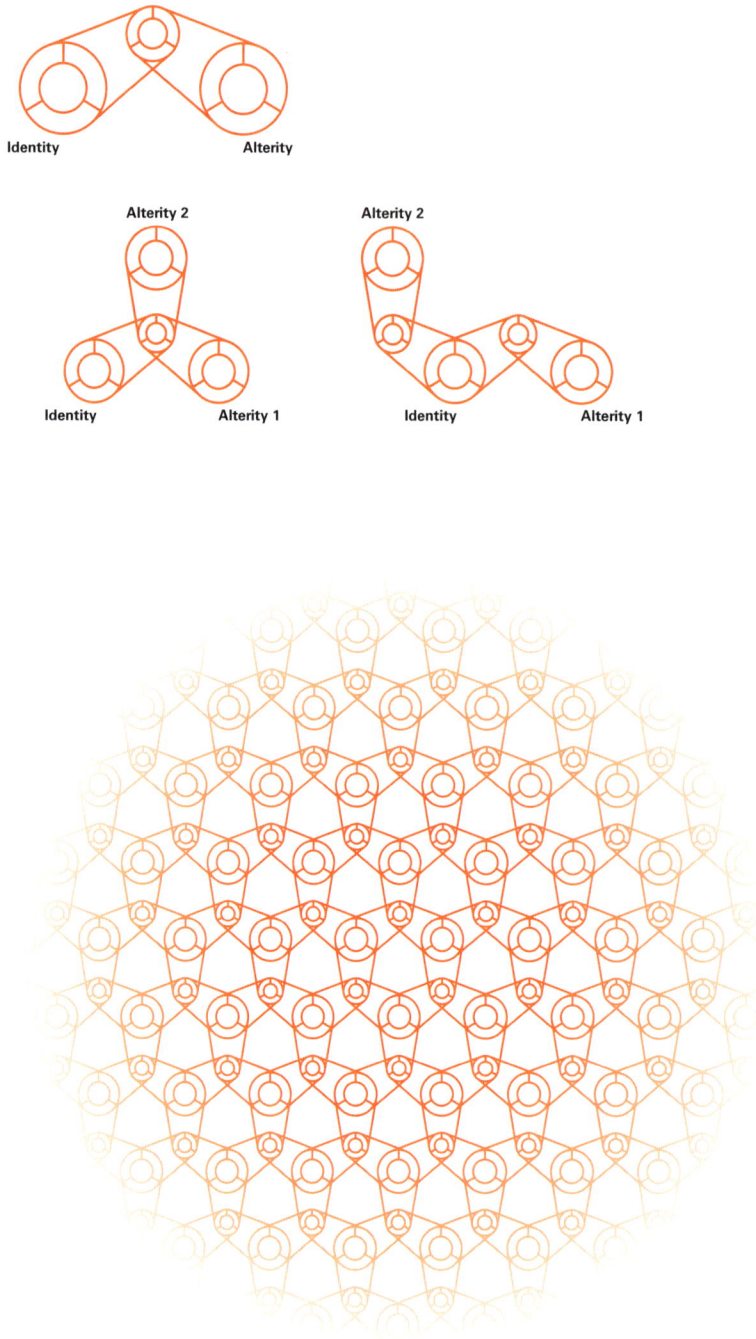

Figure 6.
Identity, alterity
and the identity
network.

Identity and value

If we now look at identities in this way, as in principle of equal mutual value, and it seems to me that we should do so in our 'network society'[3], we see a parallel of the relationships between identities (in the sense of identity and alterity) to the way networks are organised. Networks differ from 'classical' organisational concepts in that they have a different concept of hierarchy: all components of the network are indispensable to the constitution of the network and contribute their own specific value to it.

One aspect of this hierarchy is important. If a network is made up of hubs and spokes, then we will see that some of the hubs and some of the spokes are more important than others. Look at airports and the connections between them, or at the Internet and the search engines that are part of it, or at the Greenport structure of the Dutch horticultural sector. And since everyone can choose whether or not to use certain hubs and spokes, their success in terms of importance is determined not only by the value they contribute, but also by the level at which they are used — a level that can, at least in theory, change every day.

The interesting part then is, that it results possible to claim a dominant position within the network, to discern oneself and attract more 'traffic' than others. This attraction would start with showing relevance to the alterity: the counterpart should be able to discern some value of interest. Secondly, content should be interchanged, to corroborate the primary perception and establish a relationship. And finally, a certain intensity of this interaction should be reached to make the established relationship important to both counterparts.

If we look at the case of the Floriade, this is exactly what is happening here. Only when the region recognises itself as a coherent and meaningful constellation (an identity) can its constituent parts derive meaning from it and express

Note 3.
I use the 'network society' concept here as coined by Manuel Castells in the first part of his *Information Age* trilogy (Castells, 2009).

their value to the region. They will themselves recognise that they are in fact adding value to a shared network and will establish their own position within it. Local authorities will define common ambitions and behaviours, horticultural entrepreneurs will promote themselves as part of a specialised and highly developed regional offer, planners and developers will adapt to the 'conduct principle' of vitality in order to maintain the harmony of the region's physical environment, and all constituents of the region will understand the value of developing and participating in the GreenXChange concept as a logical next step. Each of these constituents is needed, has its position and value in and for the network, is recognised by its counterparts and therefore exists. Once these mutual values are clear, we can begin to exchange content and conduct transactions and, over time, achieve a certain intensity in doing so.

Now we can go one step further: if value is created within the network through object-oriented contact, and if the network in its appearance can serve as a model for communication in general, then this is also the solution to the identity paradox described above: that each identity must constitute itself, yet must be recognised by something else in order to exist. First, there must be a self-worth of the sender, a meaning and value for the external receiver; second, there must be a content-driven dialogue; and third, there must be some degree of actual contact. In other words, a quantitative aspect can contribute to the success of the qualitative aspects of 'significance' and 'content'. The more substantial the contact, the greater the presence.

There is a difference between showing oneself and fulfilling oneself. With the current density of information, it is impossible for anyone to be aware of everything that is on offer. Therefore, each of us is armed to the teeth with defence mechanisms to ensure that only useful information gets through. And what we perceive as meaningful is determined by our own identity, our will, our ambition. But our identity, in turn, is only fulfilled in interaction with the environment. And so the optimal communication situation for any participant in communication is that of interdependence.

I define interdependence as meaningful participation in (communicative) society. We give and take, we are part of the communication to which we are partly committed. Not only to sustain ourselves, but also to move forward together. We do not claim a domain, but take our place in the whole. We do not have to shout to be heard, because people will listen, because dialogue is our common existence. Just being part of the Boskoop region makes everyone relevant to all the other parts of the Boskoop region; otherwise there would be no Boskoop region.

In Chapter 2, we will look at the basic conditions for organisations to define themselves and show their value; in Chapter 3, we will analyse the process of communicating mutual ambitions and values and how to obtain this optimal situation of interdependence.

Design Principles on identity and alterity.

We use what is already there and only add what is missing.

We interact through mutual values.

We grant and take positions in the network of which we are all part.

We are granted responsibility based on our perceived role and value.

Definition Issue I: The Paradox of the Identity Principle.

Every object is fully identical to itself.

Identity exists by the grace of recognition. Identity needs an alterity, a second instance that establishes and recognises the existence of the first. Recognition, in turn, is mutual. This presupposes a shared space, a place where one identity meets another. It also presupposes a shared moment, a coincidence between the two. And it presupposes a reference to something that can be understood: each identity must refer to the universally understandable to be seen and recognised, and to have relevance for the other. Identities are therefore naturally part of a network.
At the same time, identities are self-validating. Whether we are people or organisations, our identity says: 'I am here now, so I exist in a unique manner'. Because there is no second identity that is identical to this one. Each identity is unique, self-contained and conclusive; otherwise, it would not be an identity.
So, identities are paradoxes: to exist they must be uniquely themselves; to exist they must be universally recognisable by something else.

Discovering and showing
your value and relevance.

The development logic of
your organisation.

Technology organisation
VITO confirms its authority.

The 'identity matrix' as a
defining tool.

2

Position.

Identity can guide you.

VISION ON
TECHNOLOGY
FOR A
BETTER WORLD

Vlaamse Instelling voor Technologisch Onderzoek.
How a national institute confirmed its authority.

Developing technology for the public good is a complex matter. If it were developed solely by private parties, it would be difficult to steer the technological development of society, and all the costs of development would be reflected in the price of the resulting products or services — which might make them too expensive for lower-income target groups. At the same time, private parties would have to go to great lengths to research and understand the needs of the public in the area of technology — knowledge that is available in policy-making institutions such as governments, academia, other public institutions and NGOs. And thirdly, the public interest is a matter of political decisions, which in many cases go beyond the market-based perspective of companies, for example in the case of infrastructure, water management or energy. So what we need here is an intermediary for public-private partnerships in technology development.

Like many countries, Belgium has an independent national organisation for technological research and development to support and accelerate cooperation between the public and private sectors. The Flemish Institute for Technological Research (VITO for short) has the task of establishing relevant collaborations between private technology companies, academia and public stakeholders in order to stimulate the development of technologies that will improve the lives of the people living and working in Flanders (and, in many cases, the rest of the world). VITO has five working areas: Energy, Chemistry, Materials, Healthcare and Land Use, initiates development projects or receives mandates from public institutions, forms joint ventures where necessary, develops IP and creates spin-offs for the market.

VITO is thus a hybrid organisation: it operates in different business models, ranging from access to subsidies or other public funding (including funding for its own existence) to privatised models such as licensing the developed IP or acquiring a stake in the resulting autonomous companies that use the developed technology. As is always the case in a political environment, there is discussion about public funding for VITO itself. One of the challenges for VITO is therefore to be as self-sufficient as possible or, to put it another way, to create a value for the public domain (including an economic value) that is unquestionable. This creates a rather complex situation for the organisation, which has to position itself in no less than three areas: the public domain, the technology domain and the business domain.

In 2016, VITO approached Total Identity with the request to strengthen its positioning and communication in order to be better equipped for this challenge. The result was an extensive project, spanning several years and consisting of various phases, ranging from the definition of VITO's identity and corporate story, to a thoroughly structured and proposition-based way of communicating, linked to VITO's primary development process, as well as a rebranding and redesign of the visual aspects of communication. We worked in a large multidisciplinary team with Flemish and Dutch members from VITO and agencies in Antwerp, The Hague and Amsterdam, including designers, strategists, developers, project managers, multimedia specialists and copywriters. For this reason, we had to structure both our process and the content and objectives very strictly in order to avoid 'deviating from the brief'.

Vision and concept
We started by looking at what VITO's proposition was. Using a model that we had developed over the years, the 'Identity Compass',[4] which links proposition, ambition and time in a very structured way, what we found in the case of VITO was a creative organisation that joined up with other organisations to work on technology for a better world.
Starting with the simple insight that, at the beginning of the 21st century, 'the only growth possible is sustainable growth',

Note 4.
See the paragraph 'Describing corporate identity' further in this chapter for an elaborate description of this model.

	Identity VITO's Ambition	Brand Intended brain position	Profiling Intended recognition
Starting Point Assumptions	**Vision and mission** Sustainable growth is the only possible growth. We need feasible and profitable technology for that. VITO connects research and market, knowledge and business	**Personality**	**Force field and positioning** Cleantech in chemicals, materials and energy. Applications in healthcare and land use.
Direction Choices	**Strategy and values** Standardisation, economies of scale, increasing intelligence. Partnership with commercial parties, who can turn a good idea into a reality.	**Proposition and value creation** VITO realises transitions, converts knowledge into business models, enables choices in cooperations and chains and accelerates the sustainability transition.	**Communication themes** Spin-offs and tools. Results rather than processes.
Expression Design	**Activities and competences** We work, together with others, on cleantech in chemistry, materials and energy, by creating spin-offs that lead to successful business.	**Visualisation and tone of voice** Models, cases and explanations. The brand as a partner in processes, linkable and visible, endorser of initiatives: VITO and X are working on Y.	**Boilerplate and pay-off** Sustainable growth is the only possible growth. VITO connects research and market, knowledge and business and turns research into succesful business. Vision on technology for a better world.

Figure 7.
VITO's 'Identity Compass'.

VITO turned out to be the institute that could standardise, scale and grow smart sustainability solutions precisely because of its public mission. In other words: VITO takes public responsibility for the technology being developed, assesses its impact and promotes its sustainability.

This insight led to a new mission statement for VITO: 'Vision on Technology for a Better World'. Here, VITO positions itself as the guardian of the public interest in the technology developed together with the market, not only by ensuring its qualitative but also its quantitative impact: the results must be interesting for a private company to develop and market, otherwise they will not have the desired impact. Or, as one VITO team member put it: "If what is proposed as a technological development doesn't contribute to a better world in the long term, either qualitatively or quantitatively, then we don't do it. Because our goal is basically to accelerate the transition to a sustainable world." That last sentence made it right into the boilerplate.

On the basis of this redefined position and proposition, we began to work on communicative principles and means. To do this, we turned to VITO's primary process: what does the organisation actually do on a daily basis? Here we found a recurring pattern: knowledge is used as input to create technological solutions as output, which in turn have an impact on society and its development. For us, this was a very interesting pattern because it allowed us to see VITO in a coherent and comprehensible way. However, we had to make some adjustments and additions to turn this instrument into a positioning communication and branding tool.

Firstly, we missed the positioning of VITO as such. By working with knowledge to create relevant outputs for desired impacts, VITO emerges as the authority on sustainability. They appear to be the organisation that assesses the sustainable quality of any technology developed through public-private collaboration — precisely because they have the knowledge. So instead of a working pattern, we now saw a cycle: high-impact solutions for society require the support of an authority, and authority in turn grows with visible impact.

Then we thought about the relevance and communication of this 'work cycle'. In technology, we are very used to starting at the beginning of things: it all starts with knowledge. But we felt that VITO, with its specific proposition and mission of accelerating sustainability, needed to start at a different point in the cycle: with impact. This in turn meant that the communication of what VITO actually does had to use the reverse direction of the process itself to explain it.

In VITO's communication, we therefore proposed a very strict storyline for both the cases and the corporate communication, which always starts with the impact: what is the outcome of what VITO has contributed, what is the benefit for society? In terms of output, what did VITO need to do this, how did they

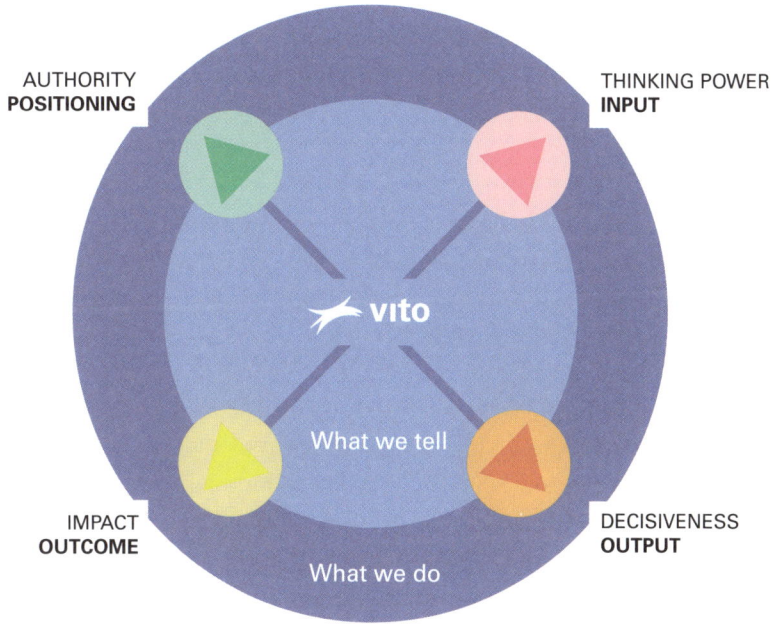

Figure 8.
VITO's primary
process
conceived as a
cycle.

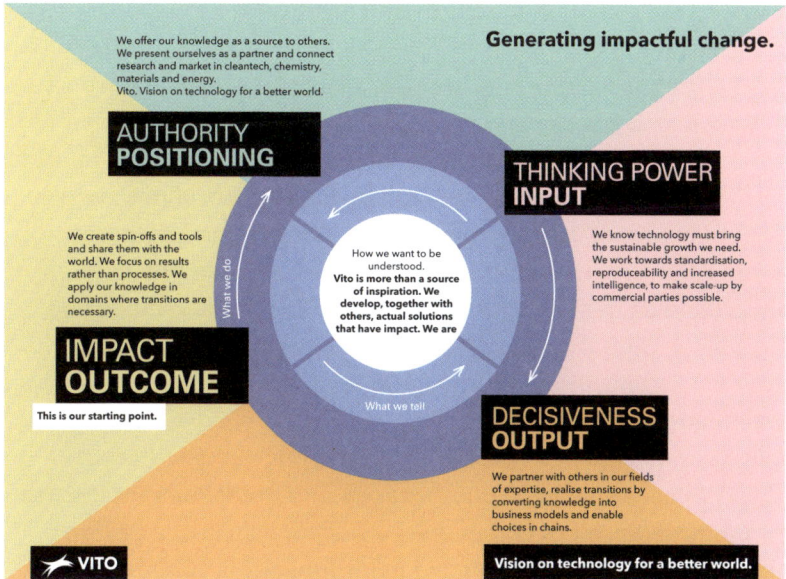

Figure 9.
VITO's
communication,
based on the
primary process
(summarised
version).

get to these results? What knowledge was used, what starting points and methods? And finally, what does this say to the world about VITO's level of thinking and action, i.e. about its authority?

The next step was to operationalise what we had discovered and structured. Here we worked in two directions: we rebranded and restyled the organisation's visual identity and structured its communications.[5]

In terms of rebranding, we came to the conclusion that both the brand itself and the visual representation of VITO as a whole needed to be refreshed. First of all, the visualisation was, with all due respect, outdated. It was based on the typical scientific approach to data presentation and had little connection to the brand, resulting in a lack of consistency in the presentation of VITO as a whole. Secondly, and perhaps more importantly, we took the view that 'if this is about impact — then let's communicate impact'. In other words, we proposed a visual identity overhaul that would represent VITO with strength, clarity, confidence — in short, with authority.

We redesigned the brand, created a coherent visual approach of brand, work areas and core messages, and a communication system that uses the storyline from impact to output to input to authority. We built on what we called 'basic storylines', which told the story of cases, projects, collaborations or corporate issues at a general and comprehensive level, and which were then used as the basis for the design of brochures, magazine articles or digital assets. We created a database of content that VITO can use again and again in all its different media and publications.

We designed a colour palette, a bold typography, different levels of consistency in photography and guidelines for the use of multimedia, all of which were incorporated into a design manual and initial examples of communication tools, such as

Note 5.
A third direction was the matter of impact in a scientific environment; basically, we worked on a model that made impact measurable and visible. The major effort here was done by the scientists of VITO themselves.

the annual report and proposals for the look and feel of the website. All of this was in line with the definition of the identity and its communication, and literally brought VITO's new positioning to life, not only by telling the story of impact, but also by showing the impact.

Figure 10.
Some examples of VITO's 'basic storylines' and their implementation in communication means.

Identity aspects

What we found very important in the case of VITO was that positioning and profiling have to do with awareness, credibility and strength. The way VITO was presenting itself at the time was not very convincing — but at the same time the level and quality of what is actually happening at VITO is very high. This incongruity led to positioning problems: only people who knew the organisation better were convinced of its quality; to everyone else (including financial stakeholders!) VITO had to explain (if not defend) itself again and again. Working together on a description of an organisation's identity is a very powerful way of forcing the organisation to reflect on itself and make it aware of its own role, quality and value — after which a review of how the organisation presents this role, quality and value is in many cases a wake-up call: 'Is this really how we present ourselves?'

Reflecting on the identity serves several purposes: it raises awareness, as mentioned above, but also provides direction at a strategic and marketing level. Once described in an inspiring way, the identity brings new energy and motivation to the organisation and the people who work in it. It makes clear what the organisation stands for, why people choose to work here, what value it brings to its environment. And it connects the organisation to that environment by demonstrating its relevance. To achieve these benefits, however, the organisation should be prepared to change not only its story and narrative, but also its behaviour. Telling a story that is inconsistent with what people experience from the organisation on a day-to-day basis is deadly; the story should be true, activated, lived. I will return to this point in the next chapter; for now, let me just say that credibility, consistency and strength are vital. An organisation's identity should be both compelling and convincing.

A second theme that emerges from the VITO case is that whatever changes and transitions an organisation deems necessary, they should be understandable both to its own people and to the 'outside world'. Let me explain what I mean by this. Suppose that, as a result of this identity formulation process, VITO had taken on a radically different position or role: the role of a ruler in the market, or that of a service organisation. Both might have been possible (though not as an ideal scenario) — but that would have made the organisation change too quickly and therefore be perceived as untrustworthy. People simply don't accept that organisations can change radically from one day to the next — because they know it's impossible. Established organisations are like large oil tankers: they change course in stages.[6]

So, in addition to taking small steps of development that people can experience as logical and natural, the organisation needs to explain why it is taking these steps. It needs to talk about its own discoveries about its identity in order to be accepted in the desired new role and position. And it should be prepared for the fact that this process of gradual change requires a clear vision of the end goal, a lot of patience, good planning and the determination to stick to the plan.

A final issue that has been exemplary in the development of VITO's identity is the need for practicality. Just as the outside world will not accept radical changes of course and behaviour, so will the staff of the organisation itself, for a number of reasons. First of all, they will be offended by the suggestion that 'obviously we have been getting it wrong all along' — a reaction that is, of course, perfectly understandable. After all, most peoplem put their heart and soul into their work, are the experts on their own situation and their own contribution, and will not accept change unless they are convinced of the need for it. The scientists working at VITO were very specific about this: science needs structure to be trustworthy. They needed to understand why things should be perceived differently from now on. Secondly, people need to be empowered to 'do' change. I will discuss the issue of change in more detail in Chapter 3, but let me just say here that organisations, work areas, teams

Note 6.
In order to initiate this change, however, a radical vision of the future of the organisation is indispensable, and some 'speedboats' might be necessary to lead the way in order to make this gradual change actually happen.

and individuals are organised in a deliberate way, based on experience on the one hand, and mission and ambition on the other. Things are there for a reason, patterns of working and thinking do not emerge for nothing. Even when people are convinced of the need to change, it is difficult to organise around that change; everything in the organisation is geared to the way it works at the moment. Organisations are machines and almost every aspect of their structure blocks change.

Change takes time, explanation and perseverance; and a clear definition of the organisation's identity and its consequences, inspiring the organisation and its environment by communicating this identity, will certainly help — but will not work miracles.

Describing corporate identity
Describing a corporate identity is a challenge if, like me, you understand identity in a multifaceted way. Identity is dynamic, interactive, organic, multidirectional... So, in my opinion, corporate identity precedes Birkigt and Stadler's sum of personality and channels, which is sometimes presented as the corporate identity itself — but actually describes its presentation. Before defining the 'communicative' aspects, we need to describe the content, the ambition, the interactive aspects and the direction of development of the corporate identity (as Birkigt and Stadler also do, of course).

Over the years, I have made extensive use of the model in Figure 11, in different variants, developing it over the years and adapting it to specific challenges and situations. It is the practical way of looking at the interaction between identity and alterity that I described in Chapter 1. The version I show here is the one we used at VITO and aims to translate identity into a controllable perception.[7] Using such a rigorous representation is essential. Working on a description of your identity is not to be taken lightly: its nature is fluid, ephemeral, intangible.

Note 7.
We will see a different version in Chapter 4.

Identity Compass	Identity Ambition of the Organisation	Brand Intended Brain Position	Profile Intended Recognition
Starting Point Assumptions	**Vision and Mission** How do we see the world around us? What part do we want to play in that world? What is our 'assignment'?	**Personality** How is our balance between individuality and collectivity, and between freedom and order? What is our 'archetype'?	**Arena and Position** Who are our stakeholders and competition? In which networks do we operate? Where do we take our stand?
Direction Choices	**Strategy and Values** How do pursue our assignment? What do we consider important? Which beliefs do we share?	**Proposition and Value Creation** What can people 'buy' from us? What do we actually offer? What is the value of our offer and how do we create that value?	**Communication Themes** Which domain(s) do we claim? In what are we thought leader? Which themes and issues confirm our value?
Expression Design	**Activities and Competences** How do we organise ourselves? What is our service design? How do we work together? What do we need to be able of?	**Visualisation and Tone of Voice** How do we represent ourselves visually and in our messages? What makes us recognisable?	**Boilerplate and pay-off** What is the shortest explanation of who we are, what we want and which value we offer? What is our added value?

Figure 11.
Identity Compass, in the version we used for VITO.

You need to reduce your definitions to their bare essence in order to understand the true character, relevance and meaning of the identity — only then can you begin to think about its development, use and representation.

Imagine working without such a tool. Your basic strategic definitions would be all over the place, as the perception of what the organisation's identity actually is would be blurred by the question of what identity is as a concept, what it consists of, how it is described and how it is decided. Your strategy would have no foundation because you would not agree on its starting point. Your brand and other communicative expressions would be off-brief because there is no clear brief. Etcetera.

Corporate identity is essentially a very abstract concept; at the same time, we usually use our gut feeling to describe it: 'This is who we are'. This will undoubtedly lead to confusion about personality, brand, history, strategy, ambition and external expressions of the organisation's character. A model like the Identity Compass (or any other well-designed model) will of course limit you to certain aspects and create its own bias, as it denies the dynamics of identity to some extent; but it is the only way to make your gut feeling tangible.[8]

Continuity and transition (Vision and Mission, Strategy and Values)
VITO was able to stay true to its mission by changing the perception of that mission — not the mission itself. The organisation confirmed its role as a link between the public, private, academic, technological and business sectors. But by discovering, defining and expressing its own purpose as 'accelerator of the transition to a sustainable world', it found a direction for revaluing this role and for transitioning the organisation without losing itself.

This is a very powerful way of ensuring your continuity: to remain yourself, you adapt to the changing demands of your environment and your own organisation, not by changing radically, but by redefining the mission you have been given, or that you have given yourself at the beginning. I will return to this aspect in Chapter 4; for now, I will consider the consequences of this kind of self-development at the level of the corporate identity of the organisation as such.

Corporate identity and dynamics (Strategy and Values, Proposition and Value Creation)
Rather than defining corporate identity as a given and static fact, I would like to take a more dynamic approach. In my view and experience, corporate identity uses its representation as an expression of its desire to exist, to have meaning for the outside world, to be relevant to certain stakeholders. It is a strategic tool, and strategy, as we know, has a temporal aspect: it aims to achieve goals in the future. Identity expresses origin, vision and ambition — not the state of things.

Note 8.
Apart from using a model, describing your identity will also ask for discipline in the use of such a model; answering the questions in the model in the manner they are supposed to be answered is vital, as it will again lead you into chaos if you don't.

Birkigt and Stadler define corporate identity as 'die strategisch geplante und operativ eingesetzte Selbstdarstellung und Verhaltensweise eines Unternehmens nach innen und außen auf Basis einer festgelegten Unternehmensphilosophe, einer langfristigen Unternehmenszielsetzung und eines definierten (Soll)Images — mit dem Willen, alle Handlungsinstrumente des Unternehmens in einheitlichen Rahmen nach innen und außen zur Darstellung zu bringen.'[9] We read 'Unternehmen' here in a broader sense: as an organisation, a plan, a project, a programme, a region et cetera, with the aim of establishing, maintaining and expressing itself; an endeavour rather than a company.

Corporate identity then represents the guiding factor in a process of working towards the defined mission. It provides a compass and a point of reference in the dynamics surrounding the organisation. In the case of VITO, if the purpose is to accelerate the transition to a sustainable world, VITO's identity makes this claim credible by expressing the appropriate behaviour and representation, while at the same time being able to respond to issues and situations. A good decription of corporate identity in this sense provides both a development dimension and a guiding principle, enabling the organisation to remain true to itself by changing in a consistent way.

Ambition and absorption capacity (Personality and Activity and Competences)

If your process of discovering and describing your identity is well organised (see also the Epilogue), you will discover more than just the bare aspects of your identity; in almost all cases you will find intuitions, biases, emotions and personal ambitions that are connected to your identity.

People, including the people who work in your organisation, have values; personal values, things that are important to them and that guide their lives, both professionally and personally. Rather than seeing these aspects as noise, blurring the strict

Note 9.
'The strategically planned and operationally implemented, internally and externally directed representation and conduct of a company, based on a defined corporate philosophy, a long-term corporate objective and a defined (target) image — with the intention to present all of the company's instruments of action in a uniform framework, both internally and externally.' (Birkigt et al, 1994, p.18.)

and general definition of identity you are looking for, you should see them as essential to your identity and the development of your organisation. They describe relationships, conflicts, issues and values that are more or less hidden or at least submerged. At the same time, discovering what's hidden in everyday work will tell you something about the support you can expect for the ambition expressed by your identity. You may want to go somewhere as an organisation, but do the people who make up the organisation also want to go there? Can they cope with the scale and speed of change, development and shifting insights?

In other words, ambitions can only be realised if you have a thorough understanding of the scope for them in your organisation. People generally do not want to change, so you need to answer some questions before you even propose change: How aligned is everyone? Will it be possible to convince everyone of the need for change? Why do people work in your organisation? Are their personal values aligned with the organisation's values? What will inspire them? What are their change styles? In short, the less tangible aspects will tell you what your organisation can 'absorb': is the development you are proposing 'doable' for the people in your organisation? How quickly, and what support will they need?

The VITO Board, leading what is essentially a scientists' organisation, had the challenge of convincing very intelligent, professional and autonomous people of the need for change. It was essential to use a very clear vision that people would recognise, an inspiring visualisation and narrative of VITO's future and its position in the world, to make clear and respect what everyone's contribution to that future and position will be, while at the same time listening very carefully to the objections raised, understanding where they came from, and responding to those objections by incorporating them into the proposals for identity and communications. We will discuss 'alignment' in Chapter 3 and 'change' in Chapter 4.

Promise and assignment (Visualisation and Tone of Voice, Boilerplate and Pay-off)

We will discuss the link between the organisation's external promise and the resulting internal mission in more detail in the next chapter, but let me mention here that the magic word is 'consistency'. The quality and ambition that you recognise 'inside' must be reflected 'outside'.

As mentioned above, the presentation of VITO was, to put it mildly, not very consistent with the potential and value of the organisation we met and analysed. The same goes for the development of the organisation: VITO, which has a great responsibility towards society, should be very trustworthy. That's why it can't change radically and overnight; people need to be able to follow what's happening. In other words, VITO must remain true to itself as it develops. A very powerful tool in this area is to see the organisation's promise to the outside world as its 'assignment' to the inside. This will be an important topic in chapter 3.

Relevance and positioning: leadership and responsibility (Vision and Mission, Arena and Position)

To a certain extent, every organisation is free to choose what it does. Anyone who makes an effort creates space for themselves. Anyone who sets up or runs an organisation, whether for profit or not, obviously has a goal. Something to be achieved, something that does not yet exist, added value to be created. In short, the organisation has an ambition.

In order to pursue that ambition, to achieve that goal, decisions have to be made. That is where the space is: in the pursuit of the goal and the path to get there. But if that is the space, then it is not clear in advance what the choices to be made will be. After all, both the goal and the path are new. And the social and business context, the network of which the organisation is a part, plays a major role in determining what is wanted and possible, in what the balance is between space and ambition.

VITO is a public organisation, largely funded by the state because of its value and role for society. The organisation's task of bringing together science and business in order to make innovations and technological developments viable and feasible, which otherwise would not come to life, is a great responsibility (and not only because society pays for it). However, the way in which VITO fulfils this mission is not prescribed. The organisation is free to choose its objectives and define its ambitions.

Completely free? No. The choices that any organisation makes are ultimately determined by its purpose, the ambition with which it was founded. Without that ambition, the organisation makes no sense. And if that ambition is not guiding and all-encompassing, then the organisation has no shape.
So, if the aim is not just to achieve success as such, but to do so successfully, then the organisation must do nothing more than remain true to itself. Not by ignoring the environment or even taking it for granted, but by creating sufficient connectivity and interaction between its ambition and the environment. By being aware of its own driving force and significance, by developing and sharing initiatives that are relevant, by choosing a modus operandi that is more than acceptable. By responding to the interests of the environment, but without distracting from its own objectives. By taking a position in the social debate and justifying its choices on the basis of ambition. By taking co-creation with its environment seriously, but retaining the initiative. By sometimes being misunderstood in its innovative power and ultimately convincing through absolute authenticity.

By staying true to the organisation's identity and communicating it carefully, VITO takes its responsibilities very seriously and becomes a trusted leader.

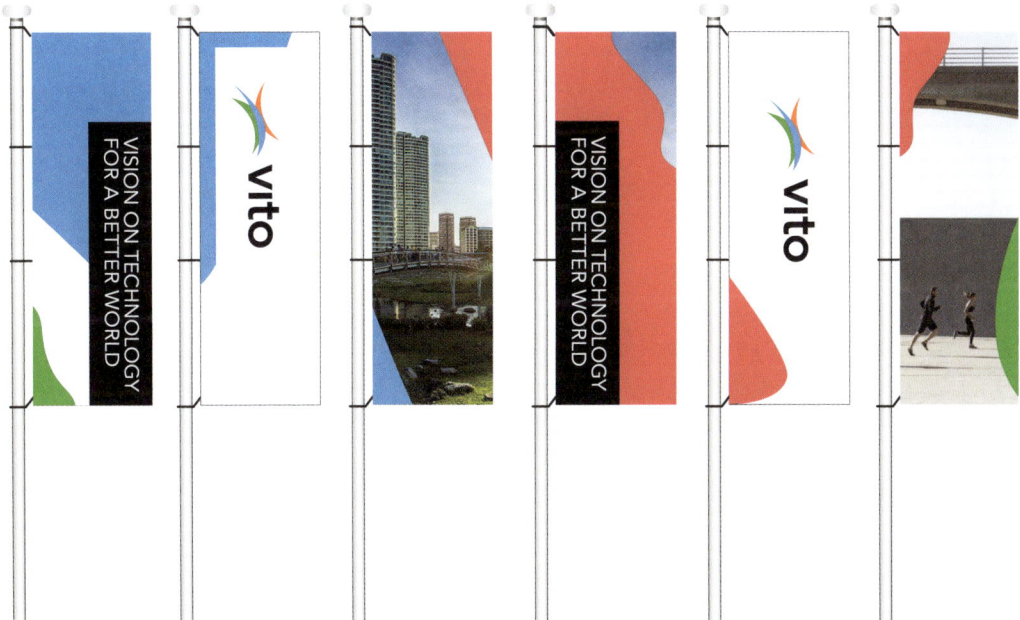

A corporate identity description needs to combine ambitions, values and interactions.

In order to remain true to ourselves as we change, we must view our organisational identity as dynamic.

We take care that both our environment and we ourselves understand our moves.

We keep in mind that the consistency between what we offer and how we present that is vital for our success.

Definition Issue II: Significance and development

We grow towards ourselves.

Rather than perceiving identity as an autonomous element, we will always discover that identity is a guideline for our development, that it has always been and will always be this guideline. The story of any organisation, its corporate story, is hidden in its origins. We start with an ambition, learn along the way what makes us who we are and what that means for our next steps. Over time, we discover our own meaning and become better able to act accordingly.
The development process of the organisation is therefore reflective: by looking at the environment and its own role, the organisation gradually gets to know itself and to actually play its desired role.
Strategic objectives are to be found in the identity aspects of the established ambition — not the other way round.
Development is a process of growing awareness of one's role in relevant challenges, of continuous appropriation of themes and issues, a voyage of discovery that consists of interpreting, shaping and giving sense, of gradually becoming more aware of oneself.

Identity and your future.

The use of a conduct principle.

How the Tergooi hospital activated its ambitions.

Identity and labour market strategies, branding policies and brand architectures.

3

Identity can share ambitions.

wij zijn er.

tergooi

Tergooi zorgt vooruit.

Tergooi.
How innovation became key for a hospital's success.

The healthcare sector in the Netherlands (as in many other countries) is going through a difficult phase. The challenges are that in the near future there will be more and more elderly people in relation to the productive population (due to the baby boom combined with longer life expectancy), technological innovation is driving up costs, and the nature of the sector is such that it is not able to increase its efficiency quickly: we are talking about real people being cared for by very dedicated other real people who are used to solving problems literally at the bedside, which makes it difficult to look at the longer term. In 2006, the sector was privatised to some extent, based on the liberal belief that introducing market dynamics and competition would reduce costs and improve quality.

This has resulted in a very complex system: health insurance companies contract healthcare from providers and make a competitive offer to users. Quality and market dynamics are monitored by an independent authority (the 'NZa'), insurance company proposals by another authority (the 'ZIN'), and policy issues and development by the Ministry. In competition with public hospitals, private companies offer (limited) healthcare services; in turn, public hospitals develop more efficient services in order not to lose production volume. Every year, there are disputes between healthcare providers and insurance companies about the volume of contracted healthcare (the so-called 'ceilings'). In 2022, an 'Integrated Healthcare Agreement' was signed by providers in the different healthcare sectors to achieve a more optimal situation and distribution of pressure and to stimulate the development of 'value-based healthcare'. There are various and complex funding and subsidy schemes for the transition of procedures and organisations. In most cases, medical specialists are not employed by the hospital, but are organised in private partnerships that work with the hospital, a construction that creates all kinds of governance complexities... In short, the organisation of our health sector in many ways makes life quite difficult for people working in the sector.

'Tergooi' in Hilversum and Blaricum is a medium-sized general hospital in the centre of the Netherlands. Its 'adherence area', the Gooi and Vecht region, has around 400,000 inhabitants, it employs almost 3,000 people and has around 300 medical specialists in general fields. It treats around 200,000 patients a year and has a turnover of around €300 million.[10] It has few distinguishing features, apart from a very high level of commitment by its staff to the people of the region. In other words, its significance is mainly based on its connection to its environment, but does not go beyond the region as such.

At the same time, there are other, larger hospitals just outside the immediate region with more developed specialities and greater ambitions. In the current state of the healthcare sector in the Netherlands, being a less important hospital alongside such more ambitious colleagues risks attracting attention in a way that may not be desirable. The trend in healthcare is to scale up in order to cut costs, by merging or cooperating very intensively. And Tergooi, which derives its strength from a deep understanding of the people in the region where it operates, could then be forced to play a different, less desirable role than it does today, thereby losing that very strength.

As a result, the hospital's board was looking for support to position the hospital more strongly. Rather than seeing this as a survival strategy, the board was looking for ways to raise the ambitions and make the hospital more relevant outside the region, as this would strengthen the revenue model and provide a firm foundation for the hospital in a broader sense: as a trusted partner in healthcare, an attractive employer, an indispensable part of the region. When we came in (in 2012), the brief we were given was quite short and simple: 'We need a pay-off'. What we ended up with (in 2017) was the result of a long, constructive and inspiring relationship in which we repositioned and renamed the hospital, renewed its visual and communicative presentation, helped build an even stronger

Note 10.
I describe the state of things during our collaboration from 2012 and 2017; since then, various things have already changed again, e.g. in 2020, the hospital added 'MC' to its name. Figures mentioned here are those at the start of our collaboration in 2012.

culture and engagement, and supported and co-developed
a number of innovative initiatives. Rather than positioning
Tergooi as a hospital, we created a more general healthcare
brand that attracted and connected other initiatives and players
in the region, giving Tergooi a significance that transcended the
'second-line healthcare' proposition that a hospital usually has.

But let's start at the beginning. When we first met, the hospital
was called 'Tergooiziekenhuizen' ('Tergooihospitals') and had
a not very appropriate, inconsistent presentation. The plural
name was a result of the merger of two former hospitals in the
Gooi and Vecht region and the desire to position the hospital
firmly in the region. Our first comment was that if the hospital
was looking for a more ambitious character, a name that
referred to its past was not the way to go. At the same time, the
general character of the hospital and its comparatively small
size provided optimal conditions for adopting an innovative,
strongly future-oriented, perhaps even experimental character;
after all, this was a controllable, consistent organisation with
highly committed people working in it. And thirdly, a more
innovative approach and character would also provide the
opportunity for new revenue models, which were needed as the
hospital was making a loss at the time.

We achieved two results at the beginning of our collaboration:
we rebaptised the hospital simply 'Tergooi', leaving room
for other propositions and values than the strict 'hospital'
or 'second-line healthcare' ones; and we created the pay-off
'Tergooi zorgt vooruit' ('Tergooi cares ahead') to immediately
point everyone in the right direction. The pay-off was
formulated in such a way that it served as a 'conduct principle'
— see later in this chapter. We defined and explained the
context and background of these choices in a policy plan based
on a simple graphic of four 'care pathways', showing the pivot
in thinking from 'proposition-centred' to 'demand-centred'.
We then worked on the hospital's presentation. We created a

Tergooi zorgt vooruit.

Figure 12.
Top: the new brand and the pay-off / conduct principle.
Middle: introductory campaign examples: 'We are there', 'We walk along', 'We live along', 'We think along'.
Bottom: the proposition worded as four 'care paths'.

brand that was ambitious and deliberately under-explained, and designed a visual and communication system and tools (from annual reports to websites) that made everything the hospital would do recognisable and consistent; again, to create opportunities for a broader and more ambitious proposition.

With the ambition and desired position defined, it was then time to look at the environment in which this ambition would play its part. We created a 'region vision': a document describing Tergooi's and its strategic allies' vision of adherence and sector developments. We used four perspectives: that of the patient, the referrer, the insurance companies, and the staff and medical specialists, and responded to these perspectives in terms of strategic choices, possible alliances and chain collaborations, and initiatives that could be developed. This region vision, together with the policy plan, became the framework for the hospital's development.

Now it was time to involve and engage the employers and medical specialists. There were two reasons for this: to create support for the direction the hospital was taking, and to respond to the challenges of the labour market. As a primary tool, we developed a programme to introduce a 'code of conduct' under the name 'Typerend Tergooi' ('Typical for Tergooi'). We elaborated the central conduct principle ('Tergooi cares ahead') into sixteen principles for specific dimensions of daily work: a consistently welcoming approach, transparency, empathy and added value to the medical treatment, translated these into tangible and useful items such as booklets and calendars, and produced (together with Maarten Corbijn) a short film 'Zorgen' ('We care'), which communicated the value of the desired commitment and behaviour on an emotional level and in its significance for the patients.
We also focused on the labour market, as a major challenge for the healthcare sector is the lack of personnel. We described the relationship of employees and medical specialists with Tergooi

as a series of 'psychological contracts' (in addition to the formal employment contract) and created personas to effectively address the ambitions and agendas of the target groups. Based on the results, Tergooi was then able to link the internal behavioural programme to external labour market campaigns.

The immediate surroundings of both Tergooi sites are very green and offer all kinds of opportunities for a so-called 'healing environment'. When we arrived, the hospital was already planning a new building at the Hilversum site in the middle of this green area. Several perspectives were combined here to show the hospital's ambition: we challenged Tergooi not only to comply with sustainability regulations, but to actually build the first energy-neutral hospital in the Netherlands. We used the 'making of' of the new building to raise awareness of sustainability and to make an early start: What are we promising to do now? And we supported Tergooi's ambition (on a conceptual and strategic level) not only to build a hospital, but also to create a 'care park' in which health and care institutions could work together and create a joint, integrated care offer for several target groups: first, second and third line care, housing, day care, etc.[11]

The adoption of an innovative character, which was Tergooi's ambition from the outset, was eventually translated into the development of so-called 'studios'. As Hilversum is the media city of the Netherlands, the combination of cure and a place where new perspectives could be developed seemed to fit naturally into this concept. A studio has two main aspects that made it an interesting way of thinking: it provides a space for developing something new, for exploring possibilities, for trying things out, and it creates value by then publishing, transmitting the results and connecting with the outside world. A studio exists by the grace of production in both senses. A natural place for innovation, we thought. We chose perspectives from the policy plan and the region vision and turned them into

Note 11.
The new buildings were inaugurated in 2023; the 'care park' was in the end not realised.

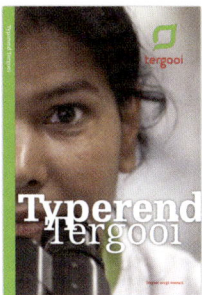

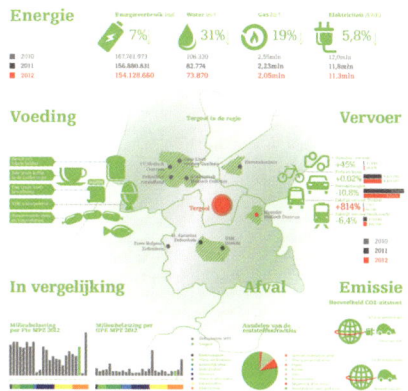

Figure 13.
Top: examples from the internal 'Typerend Tergooi' campaign.
Bottom: Tergooi's 'Sustainability Promise'.

concepts such as the 'Gezondheidsstudio' ('Health Studio'), which focused on prevention and lifestyle, and the 'Diagnosis Studio', which looked at the function of pre-medical diagnosis in a different, innovative way.

The last thing we did was to put everything we had developed together: how did it all fit together, how did we measure effort and progress, how did we make sure it was understandable to patients, stakeholders and staff? We did several things: we looked at a different approach to processes in the hospital, inspired by the famous case of the Karolinska University Hospital in Sweden, and created what we called 'patient pathways': a combination of introducing patient groups rather than medical specialties, and patient journeys rather than the more traditional processes. Responsibilities would become much clearer, innovation could be developed at a more integrative, strategic level, and progress could be monitored

Figure 14. Example products of the 'Health Studio' ('Gezondheids- studio' in Dutch).

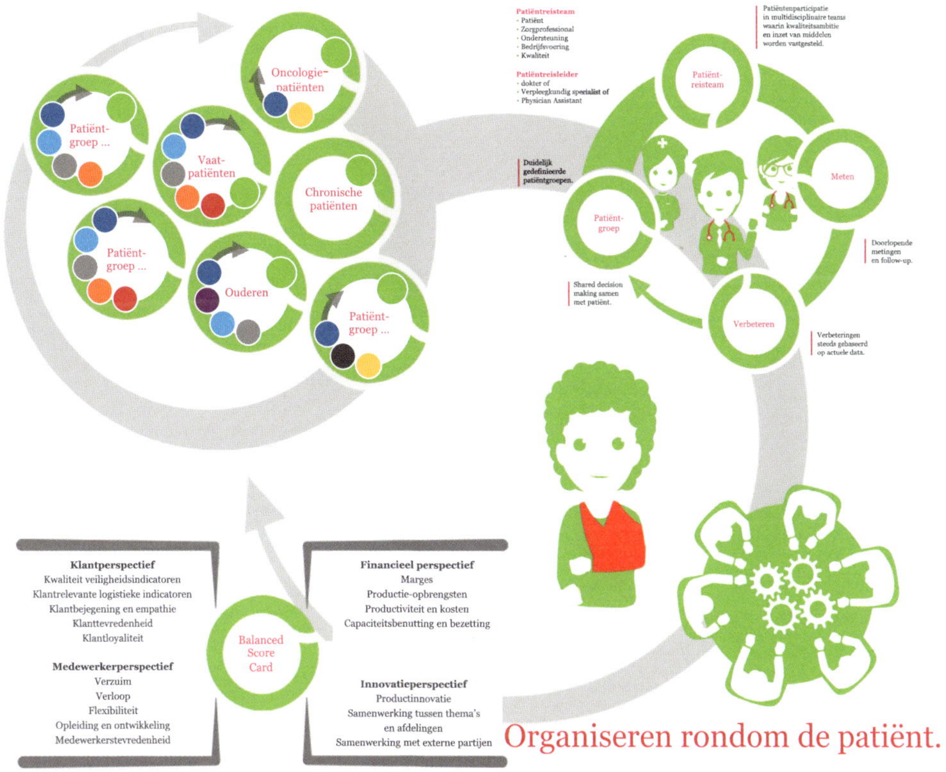

Patiëntreisteam
· Patiënt
· Zorgprofessional
· Ondersteuning
· Bedrijfsvoering
· Kwaliteit

Patiëntreisleider
· dokter of
· Verpleegkundig specialist of
· Physician Assistant

Duidelijk
gedefinieerde
patiëntgroepen.

Patiëntenparticipatie
in multidisciplinaire teams
waarin kwaliteitsambitie
en inzet van middelen
worden vastgesteld.

Patiënt-
reisteam

Patiënt-
groep

Meten

Doorlopende
metingen
en follow-up.

Shared decision
making samen
met patiënt.

Verbeteren

Verbeteringen
steeds gebaseerd
op actuele data.

Oncologie-
patiënten

Patiënt-
groep ...

Vaat-
patiënten

Chronische
patiënten

Patiënt-
groep ...

Ouderen

Patiënt-
groep ...

Klantperspectief
Kwaliteit veiligheidsindicatoren
Klantrelevante logistieke indicatoren
Klantbejegening en empathie
Klanttevredenheid
Klantloyaliteit

Medewerkerperspectief
Verzuim
Verloop
Flexibiliteit
Opleiding en ontwikkeling
Medewerkerstevredenheid

Balanced
Score
Card

Financieel perspectief
Marges
Productie-opbrengsten
Productiviteit en kosten
Capaciteitsbenutting en bezetting

Innovatieperspectief
Productinnovatie
Samenwerking tussen thema's
en afdelingen
Samenwerking met externe partijen

Organiseren rondom de patiënt.

Figure 15.
Tergooi's 'patient
pathways'.

in a consistent and transparent way. We developed a new lexicon and talked about 'patient travel teams', 'travel directors', 'healthcare value' and 'dashboards' to express the ambition to make everything that happened in Tergooi about the patient.

We developed a 'Profiling Wheel' to show the impact of everything that was developed and implemented on Tergooi's position in the network and its environment. Finally, we wrapped it all up in a comprehensive diagram we called 'The Care Continuum' to show how things fit together and where there were opportunities and gaps (see page 87).

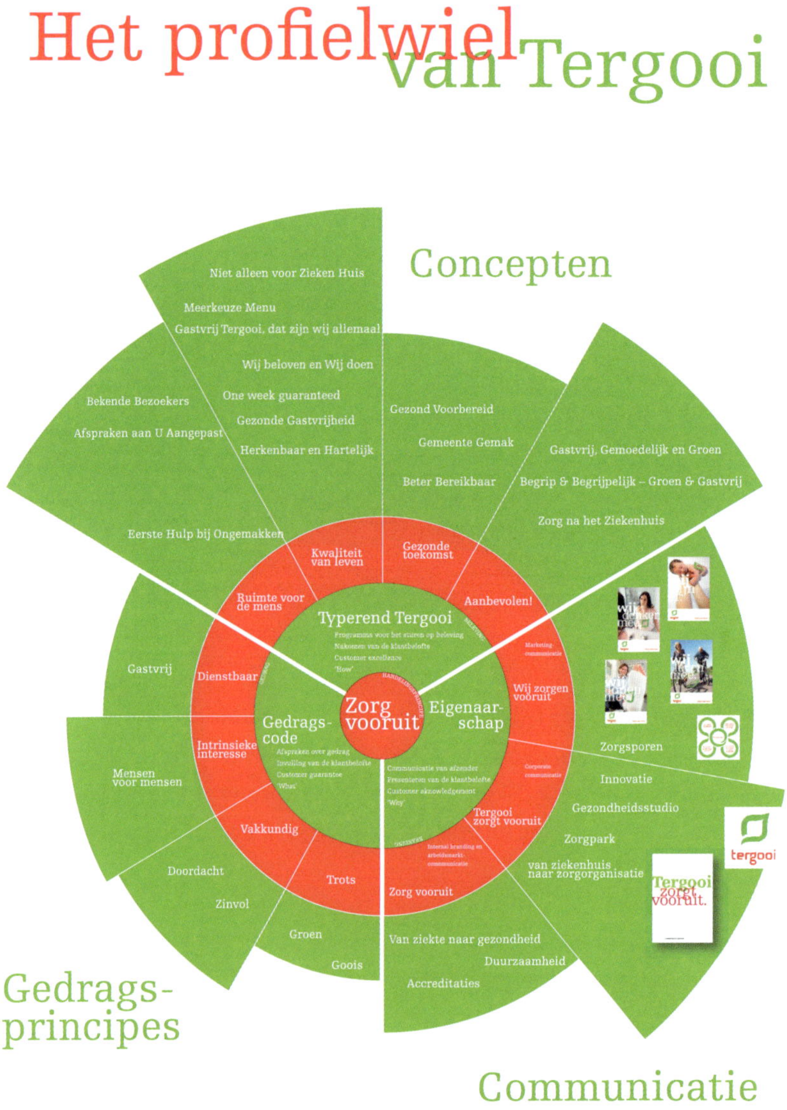
Het profielwiel van Tergooi
Concepten
Niet alleen voor Zieken Huis
Meerkeuze Menu
Gastvrij Tergooi, dat zijn wij allemaal
Wij beloven en Wij doen
One week guaranteed
Gezonde Gastvrijheid
Herkenbaar en Hartelijk
Bekende Bezoekers
Afspraken aan U Aangepast
Eerste Hulp bij Ongemakken
Gezond Voorbereid
Gemeente Gemak
Beter Bereikbaar
Gastvrij, Gemoedelijk en Groen
Begrip & Begrijpelijk – Groen & Gastvrij
Zorg na het Ziekenhuis
Kwaliteit van leven
Gezonde toekomst
Ruimte voor de mens
Aanbevolen!
Typerend Tergooi
Programma voor het sturen op beleving
Nakomen van de klantbelofte
Customer excellence
'How'
Marketing-communicatie
Wij zorgen vooruit
Gastvrij
Dienstbaar
Zorg vooruit
Gedrags-code
Afspraken over gedrag
Invulling van de klantbelofte
Customer guarantee
'What'
Eigenaar-schap
Communicatie van afzender
Presenteren van de klantbelofte
Customer aknowledgement
'Why'
Corporate communicatie
Intrinsieke interesse
Mensen voor mensen
Vakkundig
Tergooi zorgt vooruit
Internal branding en arbeidsmarkt-communicatie
Trots
Zorg vooruit
Doordacht
Zinvol
Groen
Goois
Zorgsporen
Innovatie
Gezondheidsstudio
Zorgpark
van ziekenhuis naar zorgorganisatie
tergooi
Tergooi zorgt vooruit.
Van ziekte naar gezondheid
Duurzaamheid
Accreditaties
Gedrags-principes
Communicatie

Figure 16. The 'Profiling Wheel'.

Identity aspects

One of the elements that the Tergooi case shows is the importance of consistency in organisational development. Tergooi did not disrupt itself; its most important discovery was that it had to be even more true to itself: 'If we are a hospital that literally takes care of this specific region — then let's be that hospital in the best possible way and let's stay that hospital in the future.' Tergooi's strength, as described, is its connection to the Gooi and Vecht region, with its specific population and characteristics. In other words, it was already fit for purpose. But in order to remain fit, it had to remain independent. The best way to do this was to remain true to itself. Tergooi's ambitions to become a more general healthcare brand and a more innovative organisation were therefore not revolutionary, but necessary responses to the situation. The hospital itself realised that it was by far the largest healthcare provider in the region and should therefore take the lead in building, inspiring and activating the network of healthcare providers in the region. It discovered the next version of itself through its ambitions, by asking: 'Who do we want to be for the region?'

But there's more. Ambitions inspire people. Make them want to work with you, bring their ideas, take you further. They can create a sense of belonging, of being part of a team working towards a better future. Provided — and here's the rub — they accept your ambitions as yours, they recognise you in them. You should remain you, do what you're good at, deliver what's expected of you, take the responsibility that's rightfully yours — because you are you. Ambition is one of the forms that identity can take: it is the organisation looking forward, drawing on its past, to achieve certain goals, to grow stronger, to achieve more by being true to itself. Under these conditions, people will want to be part of your ambition. Tergooi found the right answers to the challenges it faced by looking for the answers it could actually give — provided the hospital invited its environment to work together to achieve the defined ambitions.

This case also illustrates the extent to which your identity can guide your strategic decisions. Every hospital in the world faces similar challenges to Tergooi — but they are not Tergooi. For this particular hospital, with this particular history, in this particular region, with these competitors, partners, stakeholders and employees, this board has chosen a direction that has kept the organisation fit for its own specific challenges and, where necessary, made it fit for the future. At the strategic level, three major choices were made: the objective of remaining autonomous, the development of a recognisable portfolio of services to be more transparent for patients and stakeholders, and the redefinition of the offer in terms of responses to questions rather than areas of care.

To start with the latter: Tergooi offers services in four areas: prevention, acute care, chronic care and care for the elderly. For a patient, calling these services by their names is not very clear and creates quite a distance. But if you turn the domains into recognisable questions, you become immediately relevant. This is exactly what we did when we defined the four 'care pathways' at the beginning of our collaboration (see Figure 12). This strategy called for a different way of thinking, putting empathy and understanding for the patient at the heart of everything everyone does. The policy 'Tergooi cares ahead' means 'We think ahead', and the 'Typerend Tergooi' programme made the desired attitude more tangible. But all in all, Tergooi once again answered a simple question: 'Who do we want to be for the patient?' In other words, what is our identity from the patient's point of view?

For the same reason of being relevant and understandable, Tergooi decided to transform some of its activities into a portfolio of services. 'Centres of Excellence' were developed for the medical strategic priorities, the 'fortes' of the hospital, to make them more visible. The relationships and partnerships within the health network were branded to a certain extent.

In particular, the 'Health Studio' was given its own, yet well-connected, role within the hospital as a whole, and developed an intense and committed interaction with its target group. In this way, Tergooi was able on the one hand to add more general health services and develop into a broader 'brand', and on the other hand to join forces with other health providers in joint offers, without losing its own specific character and profile. Managing such a portfolio is, of course, a challenge in itself — see below for how we supported the hospital in this area. What is important here is that Tergooi once again chose to be loyal to itself and its 'customers': 'Being who we are, what can we do for our patients and stakeholders?'

The strategic choice of autonomy for the hospital had to do with the consequences of the options the hospital faced. A merger, rapid growth or too strong a strategic alliance would have had dramatic consequences for the character of the hospital: local, not too big, committed, understanding and sensitive to the population of this particular region. The hospital would have missed its purpose if it had grown too fast or had become part of a bigger picture. By choosing the position of an autonomous but strongly networked healthcare provider, it could develop without losing its character. Tergooi asked itself: 'What do we want to mean to people?'

As I said, managing a portfolio, perhaps especially for a healthcare provider, is quite a challenge. The consistency of the offer should be guaranteed, the quality of each service should be outstanding, initiatives must have a chance: we are talking about people's health. Maintaining the balance between the value of each activity in the portfolio and the integrity and consistency of the organisation's proposition can be quite difficult. After all, people who are committed to their work and their patients tend to have many ideas about how to improve and expand the organisation's overall proposition. You can quickly lose your identity. For another healthcare organisation, the 'Alrijne'

Brand and Positioning
Importance for our (market) position
Is it important to show the brand here?
Does the activity have external visibility?
Does the activity need external visibility?
Is it a typical or innovative activity for Alrijne?
Do brand and activity reinforce each other?
Does the activity offer marketing opportunities?
Does the investment outweigh the result?
Is the activitey of supra-regional importance?

Value Creation

Quality
Guarantees for the service level
Is the quality of the activity high enough?
Are we demonstrating our 'alertness'?
Is the quality of the activity consistent?
Does anybody make himself responsible
 for the quality of the activity?
Are the activity and the responsible ones
 willing to comply to the preconditions>

Care Substantive Argumentation
Importance for our proposition
Does the activity contribute to the strength of our proposition?
Is the activity necessary for profiling our proposition?
Does the activity fit in our strategy?
Does the activity exploit specific opportunities or expertise?
Does the activity encourage appropriate innovation?
Do we have confindence in the promotor and his position?
Do we stand a chance given the competition?
Is it a unique proposition?

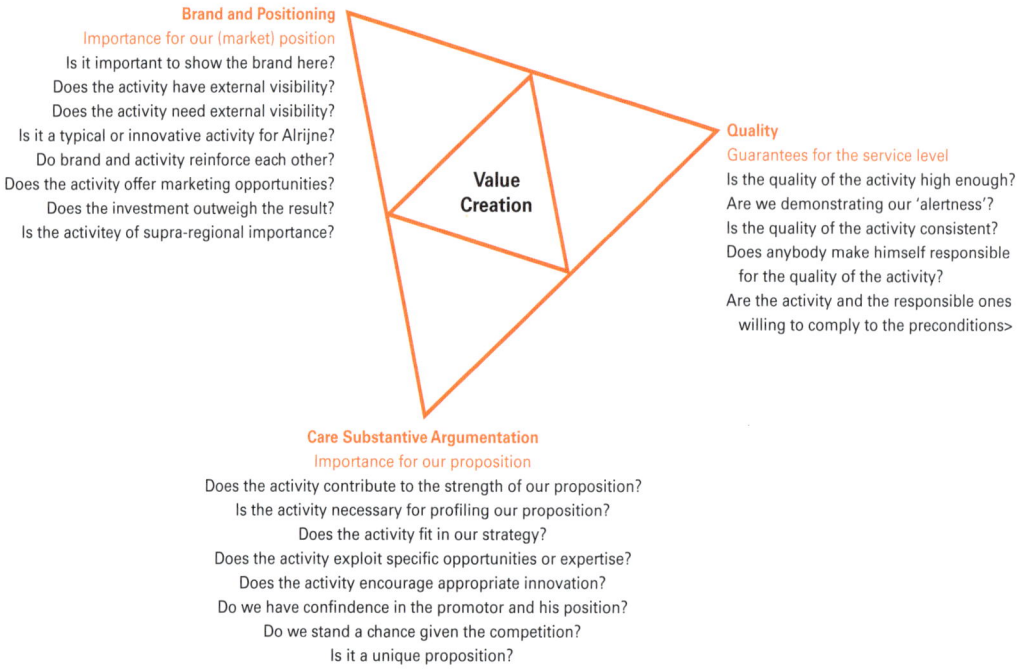

care group in Leiden, we developed a Balanced Scorecard that helped the organisation to think about every existing activity and initiative and to consider the value of the activity or initiative for the organisation and its brand — and vice versa.

A portfolio must be presented to target groups in such a way that there is no confusion about ownership and responsibility, while at the same time minimising the risk of damage to the organisation as a whole (in the event of low quality or poor performance of the activity). For Tergooi, we developed a consistent system of brands and sub-brands to achieve this (see below under 'Brand Architecture').

To conclude, basing your strategy on your identity can do a lot for you, but it does not mean that you will change much. Identity evolves; it cannot be disruptive because it would no

Figure 17.
The 'Alrijne' Balanced Score Card for existing and new activities.

longer be that specific identity. The good news is that staying true to yourself and your values is the best way to stay in touch with your environment. As we have already seen in the VITO case, you should take care to remain understandable to yourself and your environment; in this Tergooi case we can see that this actually makes you stronger. You grow in connectedness if you show a development that is truly yours, while at the same time being alert and responsive to new challenges and complexities, and keeping a sharp eye on your responsibilities. You stay relevant only by finding the right balance between staying yourself and innovating. Finding and maintaining this balance has, I think, been the great challenge for us at Tergooi.

Making identity tangible and actionable: the conduct principle
Strategies tend to be rather abstract. 'Staying autonomous' or developing a portfolio of services may be very good directions — but how can the whole organisation be empowered to implement them? Or, to put it in a more challenging way, how can your people 'do the strategy'? How can they translate the broad, abstract concepts described in the strategy into their day-to-day decisions and actions to actually move in the desired direction? Especially in healthcare, people have other things on their minds than thinking about the future and direction of their organisation. What they are doing usually requires immediate action.

What I have found to be extremely helpful is to link the overall intent of the strategy to the essence of the organisation's identity in what I call a 'conduct principle'. This is as close as I can get to translating the German word 'Handlungsprinzip', which has a very rich meaning: it describes both an operational principle and a transcendent way of thinking about those operations. 'We always do it this way' or 'This is what makes us, us'. Such a conduct principle can guide the whole strategy by linking daily actions to the overall thinking of the organisation, making it both actionable and a decision-making model.

At Tergooi, we used 'We care ahead' as the conduct principle. It made it very clear and feasible for everyone involved what the hospital was striving for: to think for patients and stakeholders, to be future-oriented, to be innovative, to be recognisable, all at the same time. It could guide everything from day-to-day behaviour: 'The floor is wet here, I'll make sure it dries because someone might slip', to big strategic decisions: 'If we are going to build a new hospital, it should be energy-neutral, because this is a big challenge for the future.'

Since both the organisation itself and the environment should have a clear picture of the organisation's ambitions, it is essential and very valuable to create a conduct principle that is clear, understandable and, above all, 'doable' on a day-to-day and strategic level. If we think back to what we said in Chapter 1 about the relationship between identity and alterity, being a consistent and recognisable factor in the network of which you are a part will give you credibility and a firm position in the network. It will create an optimal situation of interdependence between you and your environment, because everyone will know what you want, how you pursue that ambition, what value you bring to the network. It will make you trustworthy as an organisation. Imagine being inconsistent in your ambitions, having a fickle approach or not putting your money where your mouth is; it would be disastrous for your position in the network. That is where a conduct principle proves its value.

Connecting people and organisation
The key challenge then seems to be getting your people and stakeholders to 'live' your strategy and ambitions. Everyone needs to act in accordance with what has been set as the course for the organisation. Working with a conduct principle is one thing, but understanding or even feeling why we should all do so may turn out to be even more important. People should do what the strategy expects of them willingly and knowingly. They should agree with it, or even be inspired by it.

At the same time, we live in a dynamic age. In *The Corrosion of Character*, Richard Sennett describes how we have lost track of ourselves through the growing demand for flexibility: capitalism, as it has evolved, turns people into 'on-demand' factors in the production and service process, requiring them to become more and more adaptable, using temporary contracts or working with 'flexible rings' of freelancers — all the while selling this as freedom for professionals. What Sennett describes is the loss of what he calls 'character': the values and positions that individuals hold in every situation, the traits that make them recognisable and unique. Rico, one of the examples in the book, is very concerned about this, fearing that he is losing his personality and his right to play the role of a father who sets an example for his children. In modern organisations, Sennett says, we are touching on deep instincts: '(…) the new economy leads to ever-changing experiences: one is sometimes here, sometimes there, doing this today and tomorrow that. If I wanted to use some larger terms for Rico's dilemma, I could say that short-term-oriented capitalism threatens to spoil his character, especially those character traits that connect people and give each his identity.'

What Sennett does not describe is the interplay between personal and corporate identity. Rico, I believe, does not choose his employers at random, but will be attracted to organisations that appeal to him for reasons other than the opportunities and conditions they offer. Many people want to work for causes they believe are important, or for approaches they support because of their own values. I do not believe that personal values are lost, only that they mature and grow with time and experience, and that they may appear to change, but in retrospect tend to show a logical development: I see mutual value in the connection between corporate and personal identity.

In an essay I wrote with my former colleague Dennis Glijn,[12] we explored the topic of corporate social responsibility and described, among other things, the relationship between employees and organisations at the level of values. We found

Note 12.
Glijn and Van
Diemen, 2008.

WE
collective dimension

Vision

Culture

Creativity

Task of the organisation

Position

Who with whom

ME
individual dimension

In/Out

Identity

Core values

Personal values

Employees

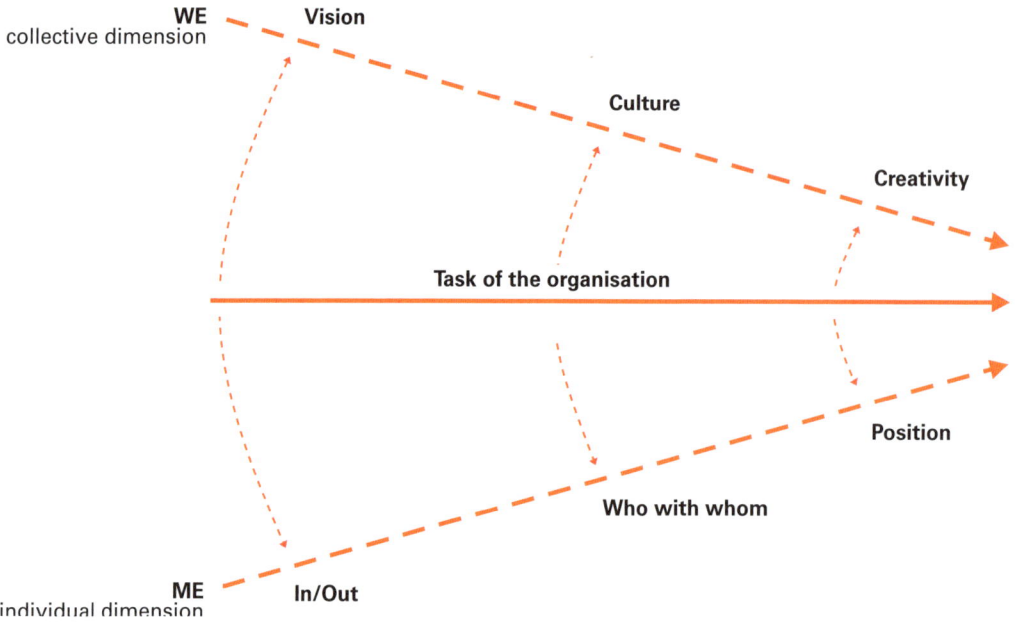

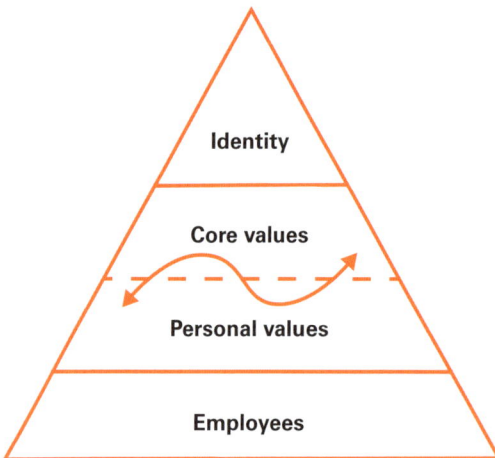

Figure 18.
Collective/
individual
dimensions
interplay and
Values Triangle.

that when core corporate values and personal values are aligned, both sides thrive because they meet each other's needs: the organisation is supported by employees, who in turn recognise and fulfil themselves through the organisation's ambitions and identity. The individual and collective dimensions are linked and mutually reinforced by an exchange of interests and beliefs. This interplay has its place at the visionary, cultural and propositional levels, and is answered by the choices that the individual employee can make as a person, in team settings and in his or her position in the organisation.

Here, by answering value-based challenges of our employees, we start building comprehensive organisations, wholes, that operate in a common direction and purpose, supported by every constituent and acquiring an aspect of beauty. Competitive, attractive organisations, conscious of their identity and loyal to the same.

Labour market strategy

In the Dutch healthcare sector (as in many other sectors), the labour market is tight, to say the least. This means that care organisations compete for employees. As working conditions are regulated by a sector-wide collective agreement, hospitals have to compete on other aspects. Location is, of course, dominant, as care facilities are deliberately spread more or less evenly across the country, but other conditions such as training, career opportunities, benefits and other material rewards also play an important role. What is striking here is that the offer to the labour market is mostly propositional: we talk about the differences between care institutions rather than about their intrinsic characteristics. Turning this around brings you back to your identity: who are you and why should someone want to work for you? The character you present to the labour market may be crucial.

But we can turn this around too. I helped one of my colleagues develop a tool to describe the 'second contract' that people have

Loyal to self *(own goals and identity)*	**I am fascinated** *(I want to grow)*	**I am passionate** *(I want to have impact)*
Loyal to organisation *(organisation goals and identity)*	**I am inspired** *(I identify)*	**I am committed** *(I want to have significance)*
	Interesting *(offers possibilities)*	Relevant *(is important)*

Employee >

Organisation >

Loyal to self *(own goals and identity)*	**I am fascinated** *(I want to grow)*	Medical specialists Specialised nurses **passionate** Management *(I want to have impact)*
Loyal to organisation *(organisation goals and identity)*	Staff **I am inspired** *(I identify)*	Department managers General nurses **committed** *(I want to have significance)* Medical support Facility staff
	Interesting *(offers possibilities)*	Relevant *(is important)*

Employee >

Organisation >

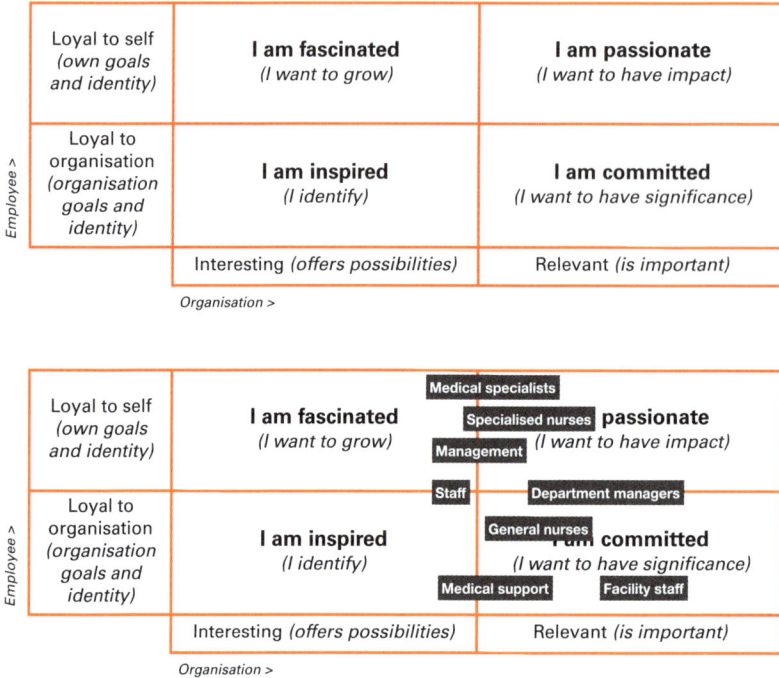

with their employer. We called it the 'psychological contract' and identified four types of contract. Individuals may be loyal to themselves (my career and circumstances are dominant) or be intrigued by the organisation's purpose and identity (my impact is dominant). Similarly, organisations can be interesting from their perspective (working there can help me achieve my goals) or relevant (what the organisation does is important to me). Four archetypes emerge from this way of thinking: the Fascinated Employee, the Motivated Employee, the Inspired Employee and the Connected Employee, as we called them.

People working in a particular sector and organisation also tend to have archetypal characteristics. Doctors are different personas from bus drivers, and nurses are different from managers. They have different agendas and aspirations. Identifying the relevant personas and plotting them in the matrix above will

Figure 19.
The 'psychological contracts' and Tergooi's plot of its relevant persona's in the model.

give you an insight into what people might be looking for in your organisation and give you more control over your labour market communications.

We did this exercise for Tergooi, starting with the hospital's ambitions and identity (after all, you are looking for people who will support you in these ambitions), describing the relevant personas and plotting them in the motivational areas above. We then developed basic text elements and imagery that would appeal to these personas and their agendas and motivations. In this way, Tergooi was able to target specific job vacancy audiences by linking its ambitions, values and identity to their motivations.

Brand architecture and portfolio

Managing your identity in terms of communication is a challenge in itself. Being a large organisation with different offers, departments, initiatives and activities, like Tergooi, means that you have to express in unmistakable messages who you are, what you do and how everything relates to each other. Some activities will be core activities, others will be more distant, supportive or even experimental. That is one side. The other side of how to show the coherence between everything you do has to do with the market you are in and the position you have or aspire to have. The combination of these two perspectives leads to strategies that are most often expressed at the level of branding. We see these strategies elaborated in so-called 'brand architectures'. In general, we can identify four models for these architectures.

The monolithic approach is widely used in markets where scale is important. You become a market leader by being the biggest in some aspect (this could be sales, but also innovation, knowledge or speed). It helps to have a single brand for everything you do. The umbrella strategy is suitable if you want to conquer new markets. You use your well-known brand as a quality and identification asset in these new markets, making it dominant in

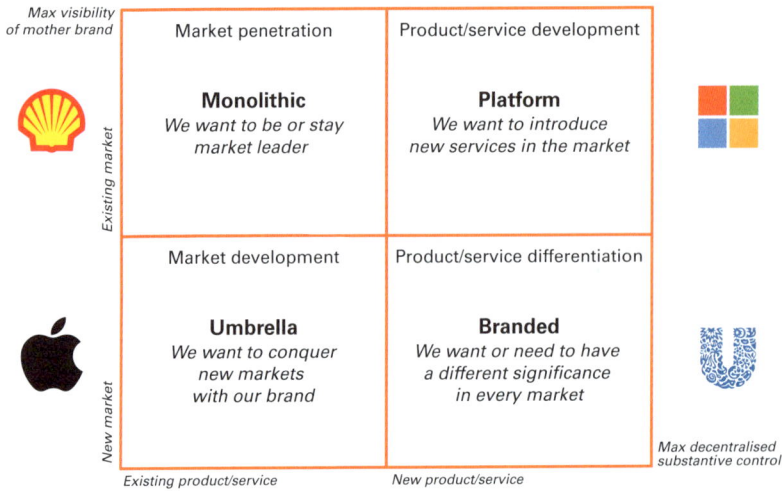

Max visibility of mother brand	Market penetration	Product/service development
	Monolithic *We want to be or stay market leader*	**Platform** *We want to introduce new services in the market*
	Market development	Product/service differentiation
	Umbrella *We want to conquer new markets with our brand*	**Branded** *We want or need to have a different significance in every market*

Existing market / *New market* (vertical axis)

Existing product/service — *New product/service* (horizontal axis)

Max decentralised substantive control

the way you name your activities. The platform strategy works well if you want to introduce new products to your market; in this case the 'parent brand' is less visible as the products themselves must be the champions; but as a potential buyer we need some assurance of ownership of the product to trust it. And a branded strategy is used when you have different challenges in different markets and work with a diverse portfolio of product and service brands to address those specific challenges.[13]

Tergooi's strategy of launching offerings at different levels made it a hybrid organisation: dominant in its regional market, a specialist in some niche markets, a developer of products and services in the healthcare sector. We translated this behaviour into a hybrid brand architecture, combining a monolithic brand for core activities with labels, sub-brands and endorsed brands for more distant activities. We developed a checklist of questions to determine which activity belonged where in this architecture, and designed a visual system to show the connections and distances between all activities and initiatives.

Note 13.
The strategically educated reader will of course recognise the Ansoff matrix in these architectures.

Figure 20.
Brand architectures.

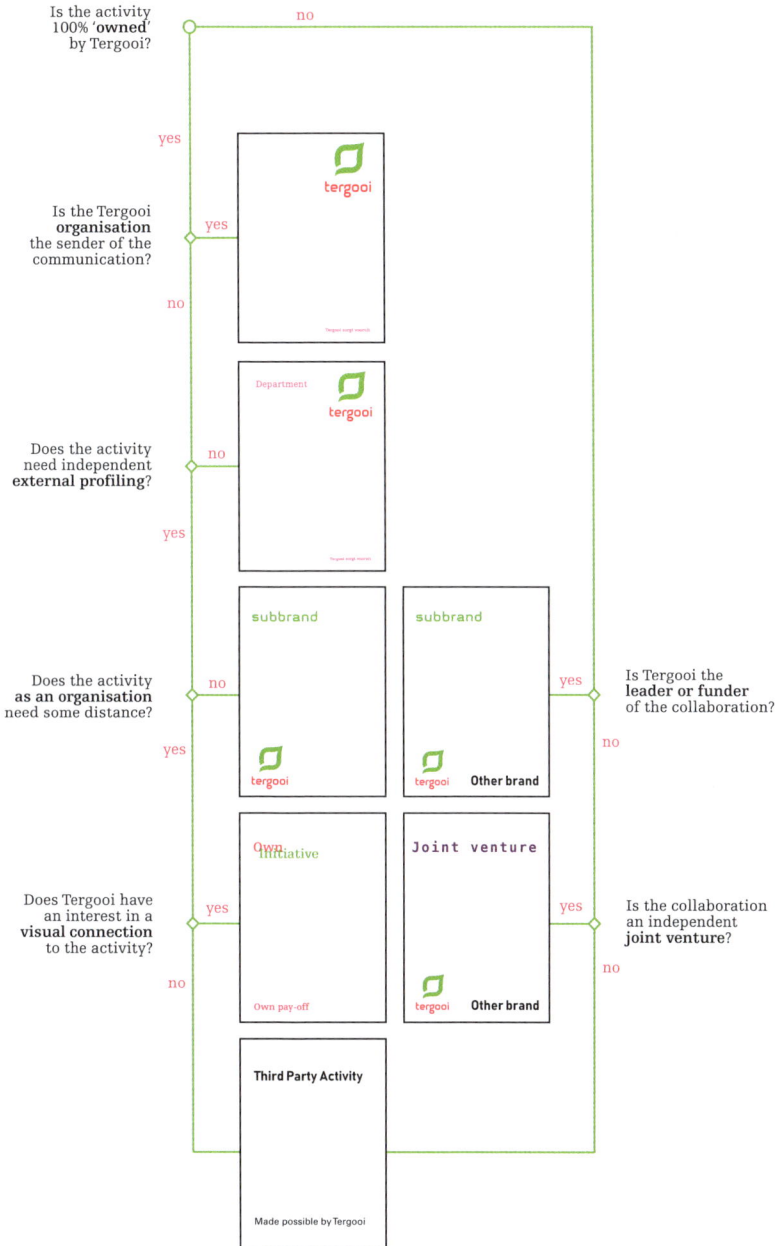

Is the activity 100% 'owned' by Tergooi?

no

yes

Is the Tergooi organisation the sender of the communication?

yes

no

tergooi

Department
tergooi

Does the activity need independent external profiling?

no

yes

subbrand

subbrand

Does the activity as an organisation need some distance?

no

yes

Is Tergooi the leader or funder of the collaboration?

yes

no

tergooi

tergooi   Other brand

Own initiative

Joint venture

Does Tergooi have an interest in a visual connection to the activity?

yes

no

Is the collaboration an independent joint venture?

yes

no

Own pay-off

tergooi   Other brand

Third Party Activity

Made possible by Tergooi

Figure 21.
Decision model on the Tergooi branding architecture.

Managing complexity

It is vital for any identity to remain comprehensible, understandable and manageable. For Tergooi, we developed a large number of initiatives and strategies, and some stakeholders may have been dazzled from time to time. What was Tergooi up to? What did all these activities, structures and initiatives mean? This is a common occurrence when developing an identity-based strategy. One of the reasons people may feel insecure is that the organisation's identity is, of course, at the root of it. Thinking about it will touch on deep beliefs and feelings. So in the final phase of our work together, we created several visualisations of how it all came together.

Figure 22 is one such visualisation. It shows the connections, places, added value and contributions of each line of thought and strategy we had developed, and links them back to our very first, fundamental idea of the four 'care pathways'.

It reassured everyone that not only were we still on track and still working for the same thing, but also that this was still Tergooi. After all we did, Tergooi was still the healthcare provider for the Gooi and Vecht region. The only thing we had done in our collaboration was to look ahead and make sure that it would stay that way in the future. Tergooi had prepared itself for new challenges by remaining itself. Once again, this is what identity can do for your strategy.

Het zorgcontinuüm van Tergooi

gezondheidsstudio

Diensten en producten rond gezondheid.

Gezondheid
Preventie
Gedrag
Lifestyle
Advies
Begeleiding
Monitoring
...

Typerend Tergooi

Care
Chronisch
Ondersteuning
Transmuraal
Integraal
Mogelijkheden
Ketenpartners
...

Virtuele inrichting

Ketens rondom concrete vragen van de patiënt.

diagnosestudio

hoe blijf ik gezond?

hoe leef ik zo lang en zo goed mogelijk?

de zorgvrager

hoe word ik weer voor gezond?

hoe leef ik met ondersteuning?

Regiovisie
Platforms
Associaties en allianties

Cure
Behandeling
Moment
Verblijf
Focus
Samenhang
Vraagsturing
...

Uitmuntend Tergooi

Care
Monitoring
Ondersteuning
Thuis
Regie
Verbindingen
Nazorg
...

Fysieke inrichting

Een plaats voor efficiënt en aangenaam bezoek en verblijf.

Inrichten en invullen van het zorgcontinuüm.

Centers of
Excellence

Figure 22.
Tergooi's 'Care Continuum', showing the interrelationships between all existing and new activities we developed.

We generate common conduct principles instead of rules.

The promise we make to the world is our daily assignment.

By sharing our ambitions, we project our values to the world and ourselves.

In our corporate strategy, we rediscover and recreate ourselves.

We make our identity ultimately recognisable to bring everybody together in a common cause.

Creating real value

Many see identity as a competitive concept, a basis for distinction. That is like saying we take the value of what is around us as the norm for what we ourselves want. It makes our organisation a result of the influences of our environment. What happens if we dare to see ourselves as the source? If we trust our own strengths? Then we offer ourselves opportunities we didn't have before. We do not look at others, we make others look at us. We enforce a certain perception of our value and do not ask for space for it, we just take it. We will connect with the world through relevance. That's one thing.

But more importantly, we want to have real value. Not in competition, but intrinsically. Not just economically, but socially, culturally and responsibly. The sustainability of our efforts depends on what real value we can add to the world. And how we, as an organisation, make ourselves fit to do so. Ultimately, we compete on beauty, on an aesthetic aspect: we become a beautiful organisation, rightful and true. And that's two.

Identity as a collective development dimension.

Responsibility and stewardship.

The example of the Gardena-Gröden World Ski Championship.

Modelling your corporate story and the interaction with your environment.

4

Ethics.

Identity can justify you.

FIS Alpine World Ski Cup Gardena-Gröden.
How responsibility lead to renewal.

In the Italian Alps, in the Dolomites to be precise, there is a very special place. To get there, you have to drive from Bolzano halfway up the Brenner Pass, turn right at Barbiano to a smaller pass and then drive through a tunnel before it opens up to you. What you will find here is a valley of astonishing beauty. Surrounded by huge, bare and steep mountains, this valley has been a well-kept secret of paradise, where the inhabitants of three villages have lived their lives for centuries. This is Val Gardena. Or is it? It is also known as Val Gardena. And as Gherdeïna...

Until not so long ago, this was a very isolated valley. The tunnels that now facilitate access were not built until the beginning of the twentieth century. Until then, you had to climb your way in and out. The valley has been quite closed off for centuries and as a result has developed its own very typical culture. It is famous for its woodwork, its entrepreneurship and the daily use of three languages: Italian and German, as is the case in most of South Tyrol, but the valley has also preserved its own retro-Romanic language, called Ladin. Hence the three names: not only for the valley itself, but also for the villages within it and for each of the mountains surrounding it.

One of these mountains may sound familiar to skiing enthusiasts: the "Langkofel" (in German), "Sassolungo" (in Italian) or "Saslong" (in Ladin). It is one of the slopes that are part of the FIS Alpine Ski World Cup series every year. It is also part of the "Club of 5", together with the "Streif" in Kitzbühel, the "Lauberhorn" in Wengen, the "Kreuzeck" in Garmisch-Partenkirchen and the "Daille" in Val d'Isère. These are the most famous, challenging and sought-after slopes for top skiers. But there is more to tell about the Saslong. It is one of the mountains where winter sports were born. The inhabitants of this valley are a hardworking and creative people who have travelled the world for centuries to sell their famous woodcarvings. On the one hand a recognisable and closed community in a valley, on the other a pioneering people. And it is precisely this mentality that has led them to pioneer the possibilities and opportunities offered by winter sports. Skiing became popular in Val Gardena after the First World War, when the local soldiers, who had practised skiing for military purposes, returned to the valley. The area proved to be very attractive for this sport, attracting skiers from other areas. The organisation of races dates back to shortly after the First World War and evolved into the first edition of the Val Gardena World Cup in 1968. Since then the event has become an integral part of the FIS Alpine Ski World Cup series, not least thanks to the innovative approach of the organisers. The event has made Val Gardena known all over the world as an attractive winter and summer holiday destination.

The Saslong is a very challenging slope and has seen famous battles between athletes. But now there are new battles to be won: the event is facing challenges that are forcing it to redefine its position and approach. Competition in the racing business is fierce, with new events appearing all the time. Winter sports are a very attractive but somewhat monolithic economic driver. Environmental issues such as global warming require new responses to traditional demands. The success of tourism development increases the pressure on the valley's fragile natural resources. The importance of the event for the economic development of the region must be maintained as an integral part of the event, but the professionalisation of the organisation is in danger of losing contact with its traditional base: the people and organisations of Val Gardena. In short, Val Gardena is worried about its future as a community, as a precious valley, as an attractive ski resort and as part of the World Cup series.

This brief description of Val Gardena is almost typical of a hero's tale: you become a hero only by overcoming challenges, including those posed by your own personality. And Val Gardena has a lot of personality. Imagine what it means to organise an Alpine Skiing World Cup! A large part of the valley's population is involved in one way or another, either professionally or as volunteers. It is a community-supported event, because people understand what it means to them and are very proud to host it. So, as they face the new challenges of the twenty-first century, they are relying on their 'pioneering tradition' and innovating as they have always done. They understand that continuity means changing from time to time. More importantly, they understand that this valley, with its awe-inspiring nature and character, is their responsibility. They have lived in it for centuries, they are part of it, they cherish every aspect of it — and they know that this now requires renewed effort. They need to be heroes again and meet the challenges they face. But where to start and where to go? The organisers of the World Cup turned to Total Identity for support.

Although our brief was defined as a corporate design exercise, it was clear from the outset that the real challenge was to position the event to sustain and renew itself. It needed to reconnect with the people of the valley and protect the environment, while at the same time offering a very strong proposition to the world of professional and recreational sport in order to maintain its position in the World Cup series. What seemed to be a dilemma turned out to be the solution: the identity of the valley and its inhabitants was the strongest guarantee of the event's continued success. All we had to do was make everyone aware of the specific values that are shared in Val Gardena, and we never had to ask for a sense of responsibility, because responsibility for the valley and the community has always been part of these values.

We took two steps before actually designing a new corporate identity: we defined the identity in terms of its meaning for the 'inside' and 'outside' world, and we wrote a 'corporate story'. For the first step, we used a different version of the 'compass' I presented in Chapter 2, a version we called the 'identity matrix'. In this version of the model, we combine themes that are

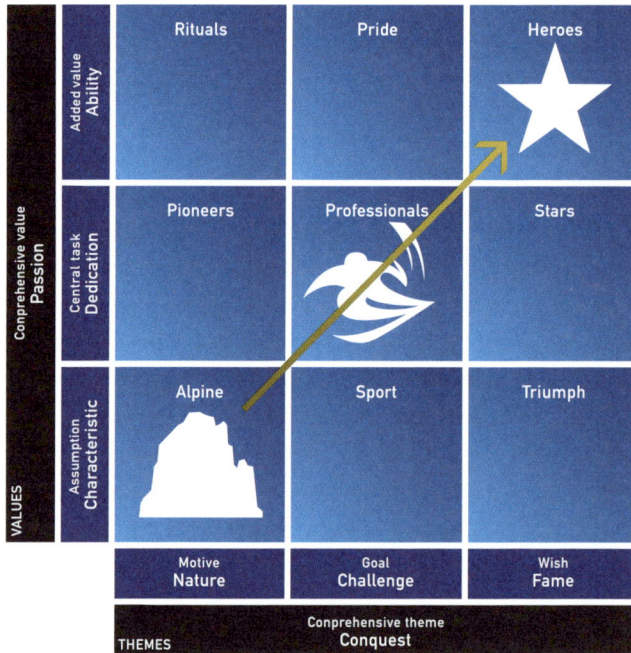

		Rituals	Pride	Heroes
Conprehensive value / **Passion**	Added value / Ability	Rituals	Pride	Heroes
	Central task / Dedication	Pioneers	Professionals	Stars
	Assumption / Characteristic	Alpine	Sport	Triumph
VALUES		Motive / Nature	Goal / Challenge	Wish / Fame
THEMES			Conprehensive theme / Conquest	

relevant to the identity's environment with core values that make up the identity from the 'inside'. What makes us relevant and what do we ourselves consider important? Filling in the matrix provides a description of the interaction between the identity and its environment. By ordering issues and values in a specific way, the matrix then also describes the developmental dimension of identity: where has it started and where is it going?

I will explain the model in more detail later in this chapter, but what became clear here was the very close relationship between the character of the valley (the characteristic alpine nature and its challenges) and its pioneering inhabitants on the one hand, and the professional sporting event on the other. The matrix shows that responsibility for the natural environment

Figure 23. The 'identity matrix' we used for Gardena-Gröden.

in which the event was born is part of the identity itself, and that pride, glory and heroism are closely linked to these natural characteristics.

We then wrote a corporate story (to which I will return): a description of how the identity is expressed and understood. In Birkigt and Stadler's model (Chapter 1), the corporate story is the link between identity and image: you control the image by telling an authentic story about yourself. But more importantly, in my view, you describe your ambition, the way you see things, the idea you have of yourself — your identity: this is how we recognise ourselves. A well-written corporate story is both a mirror and a mission for the organisation or, in this case, the region it describes. In the case of Val Gardena, the combination of community spirit and professional sporting challenge became very clear.

The original German/Italian story is about three pages long. The 'boilerplate' version (a short text that sums up and characterises an organisation or, in this case, an event and a region), which we later used as the lead text for the corporate design presentation, is one paragraph:
'The story of Gardena-Gröden is the story of a mountain, of villages near that mountain and of the people living there. But it's also a story of the development of a sport, of people who love this sport — and of course of sporters! The story tells about nature, challenge and fame. About character, dedication and ability. There are other events, and many participants — but only this one mountain. This slope creating heroes. Gardena-Gröden can make you famous.'

Of course, the corporate story, or even the boilerplate, is not appropriate for all communications; we need shorter references to who we are if we are to explain ourselves to larger and more diverse audiences. That is why we have brands, pay-offs and visuals. So our next step was to create a 'brand' for the event

[...]

Tradition bedeutet Verantwortung

Anfangs waren es noch Amateure, die sich auf einigermaßen präparierten Pisten den bestmöglichen und schnellsten Weg hinunter ins Tal suchten. Doch die Begeisterung wuchs und wuchs, und der alpine Skisport wurde bald zur beliebtesten Wintersportart überhaupt, der Jung und Alt leidenschaftlich nachging. Jedes Kind eiferte seinen großen Idolen nach, die auf immer härteren und glätteren Rennstrecken talwärts jagten. Die Weltmeisterschaft hat das Grödnertal verändert: Der Sportgeist der Grödner ist Teil ihrer kulturellen Identität geworden und bedeutete für die damalige Jugend eine reelle Chance. Eine Chance, sich von Gröden aus eine Verbindung zur weiten Welt zu schaffen. Dies brachte für die Organisatoren der Weltcup-Rennen jedoch auch eine große Verantwortung mit sich. Denn die ganze Welt blickte nach Gröden, das im Ski-Rennsport Vorbildcharakter hat. Auch vor zwei Jahren, als der Alpine Ski Weltcup sein 40-jähriges Bestehen feierte, stand Gröden — gemeinsam mit Alta Badia, das in jüngerer Zeit auch begonnen hat, Rennen zu veranstalten — im Mittelpunkt der Aufmerksamkeit. Ganz im Sinne ihres Verantwortungsbewusstseins, das sie als Pioniere im Skirenn- sport gerne tragen, haben die Grödner in Hinblick auf die Feierlichkeiten rund um 40 Jahre FIS laufend Verbesserungen durchgeführt. Die „Saslong" Strecke zählt heute immer noch zu den vollständigsten und spektakulärsten im gesamten Skizirkus. [...]

Gröden auf der Siegerstraße

Wie wird unsere Geschichte wohl weitergehen? Was wird uns 2023 erwarten? Nehmen wir einmal an, die Vorhersagen der Klimatologen bewahrheiten sich und schon in wenigen Jahren bleibt das Beten um den Schnee ungehört. Die FIS muss ganzheitlich denken und handeln und erlegt den Austragungsorten für den Ski-Weltcup immer strengere gesetzliche und ökologische Vorgaben auf. [...] Der Ski-Weltcup steht auf dem Scheideweg. Der Weltcup-Auftakt musste zwar nach hinten verlegt werden, da der Dezember einfach zu warm war, doch Gröden hat von seiner Attraktivität nichts eingebüßt. Im Gegenteil: Die Sponsoren zum Beispiel haben gerade diesen Austragungsort zu ihrem geheimen Liebling auserkoren, weil sie nirgendwo so stark in das Geschehen eingebunden werden. Überhaupt empfinden die Renngäste, Sportler und Sponsoren das Grödnertal als äußerst angenehm, da man das Gefühl hat, dass alle an einem Strang ziehen, dass die Kommunikation funktioniert und sich jeder mit dem zuweilen anstrengenden Zirkus rund um die Skirennen identifizieren kann. Die Freude am Sport wird fast greifbar mitgetragen. Gröden ist — gerade in dieser schwierigen Zeit — wieder zu einem der bedeutendsten Anziehungspunkte geworden. Dem jungen Organisationsteam ist es geglückt, die immer härter werdenden technischen Anforderungen rund um die Rennen bravourös zu meistern, da es sich stets in erster Linie um die Professionalisierung des Renngeschehens gekümmert hat. Eine Haltung, die das Publikum sehr wohl zu schätzen weiß. Die stets ausgebuchten Plätze in den Zielhängen sind jetzt noch klüger nach Sektoren unterteilt, wodurch jeder die Möglichkeit hat, beim Weltcup mitzufiebern.

Und es herrscht wieder Bombenstimmung, fast wie damals, als Stenmark vor Millionenpublikum das drittletzte Tor eingefädelt hatte. Aber nur fast: Denn schon damals lag die Kraft im Mut, Neues zu wagen — allen voran! Das ist unser Gröden.

Figure 24.
Parts of the Gardena-Gröden corporate story, in the German version.

and the valley. The event officially was called 'FIS Alpine Ski World Cup in Val Gardena/Gröden Saslong Classic' — not very concise and very instrumental; in other words, not a brand. We decided that the strongest part of this descriptive name was the part that linked the event to its origins: the valley with its specific character and culture, so from then on the event was simply called 'Gardena-Gröden'. We surrounded this name with a pay-off, a short sentence describing the added value of the brand: 'Passion and Performance', and with a descriptor, the shortest version of what something actually is: 'FIS Alpine Ski World Cup'. The pay-off unites the ambitions of the athletes, the event and the valley's inhabitants: we all work together to make Gardena-Gröden special, outstanding and unique.

Finally, we tackled the original brief: a corporate design that would position Gardena-Gröden as a top event in the competitive and recreational winter sports scene. Concluding that it was all about this one mountain that could make you a star, we blended the mountain, the star and the winning race in an appealing, festive design and combined it with the descriptor, the brand name and the pay-off. We then surrounded this brand with a visual environment that was flexible enough to facilitate the wide and changing range of media and applications, yet consistent enough to convey the professional quality we needed here. In this way, from the tickets to the hoarding, from the waysigning to the trophy, everything breathed the new ambition that had been found and showed the direction in which this event, this community, this valley wanted to develop.

Passion and Performance
FIS Alpine Ski World Cup
GARDENA-GRÖDEN

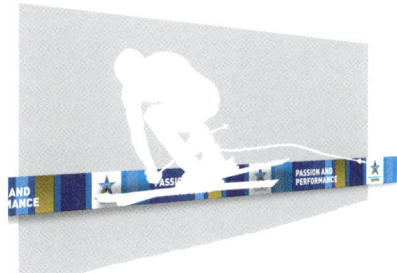

Figure 25.
Brand and
visualisation
examples.

Identity aspects

For me, the connection between origins, history and responsibility is one of the things that comes naturally to any identity. Discovering who you are comes with the responsibility of maintaining and nurturing your identity, whatever you do. This is what Sennett calls 'character': the way someone or something expresses itself in the consistency of its actions, which in turn are based on its values. The people of Val Gardena express their identity in many ways: in their culture, in the preservation of their languages, in their craftsmanship and entrepreneurship — and in the World Cup, which fits them so well. They are very conscious of their origins: the impressive natural environment that has shaped them and their culture, and they are very aware of their duty to preserve this environment. This is equally true when the origin is of a different nature, such as a man-made creation like an organisation, an artistic culture or a sector that employs many people. Rather than calling this an ethical duty, I would call it the ethical aspect of identity. Ethics are part of any identity. We are all stewards of what we create, use or develop, otherwise we would cease to be who we are.

To do this, of course, we need to be aware of the characteristics of our identity. The first step is to discover what it consists of, what logic it contains. Only then can we maintain and develop our identity. Writing your corporate story (see below) is a valuable tool for this, as it literally links origin, development and future in a tangible way. That is why we have used this tool in Val Gardena: not only to make everyone recognise themselves, but also to discover the next steps to be taken in order to remain faithful to the identity of the valley and the event.

Inspiring highlight for development

When I described the Gardena-Gröden World Championships as 'fitting' for the identity of the valley as a whole, I was referring to its competitive character, based on the natural challenges that the valley offers. These are the same challenges that have shaped the people and culture of Val Gardena and made them the heroes of their history. The identity matrix (see below) reflects this character very well. But there is a second aspect: the annual creation of the event is a community effort that brings together almost everyone in the valley. This makes the event itself a celebration of what the people of the valley have to offer the world: this is who we are, this is what we can do and we are proud of it!

Communication of this kind of events is very specific. On the one hand, there is the time factor: the event lasts two days and has to be announced, carried out and evaluated in a very short period of time. On the other hand, there is a lot of competition between events, all trying to attract as much attention as possible. Finally, there are very different target groups: the volunteers and collaborators who make the event possible and who need to be rewarded and stimulated; the participants, who need to be attracted to the event; the sponsors, who need to be persuaded to invest; the visitors, who need to experience an integrated environment during the event; the television audience, who need to see a recognisable event; and, last but not least, the spin-off target groups, mainly tourists, who need to be attracted to the area where the event takes place in order to come and ski...

Reaching all these audiences requires a wide range of communication tools, from press releases to online bookings, from TV guides to banners along the course. Consistency is essential and can only be guaranteed if the communications approach is built as a toolkit, combining the event's corporate story, communications strategy and design elements. Only then can the pride and joy of creating the event be shared with the world, making the event and the venue special and attractive to all target audiences.
An interesting aspect is the reciprocity between the event and its origins. It could not have developed its specific character in any other place: this culture, these circumstances and these

challenges make it unique, outstanding, make it Gardena-Gröden
— the event; and it rewards the valley with the presentation of
this uniqueness, of this excellence and of the specific character
of Gardena-Gröden — the valley. The event is a source of
inspiration for the development of the valley, just as the valley is
a source of inspiration for the event.

Choices
In this development, choices had to be made (and still have to be
made). Some of them were forced by inevitable developments,
such as global warming or the competition between Gardena-
Gröden and other events on the Alpine ski calendar. Some of
them seem to be made freely, like the restoration of the close
relationship between the event and the community. But in my
opinion, and in this case too, choices about identity are never
free. They depend, once again, on the close relationship between
origin, development and responsibility on the one hand, and
on the space given to the organisation on the other. Let's take a
closer look at this last aspect.

When it comes to understanding the dynamics between imposed
and 'freely' made choices, a model-based representation of how
the space for choice works can help the organisation to follow a
path that is appropriate to its ambition and character, and that
makes the organisation consistent and recognisable over time.
The basic assumption of this model is the relationship between
freedom of action and the amount, frequency and density of an
organisation's interactions (what I described in the first chapter
as the quality and quantity of interactions in the network of
identities and alterities). Many organisations seek the space
offered by their environment and become more responsive
to public opinion as they increase their interactivity with that
environment. Behaviour that Kim and Mauborgne call 'red ocean'
and that I call 'social space' (see Figure 26).
What is shown here is the extent to which the organisation feels
able to make its own choices in relation to the extent to which

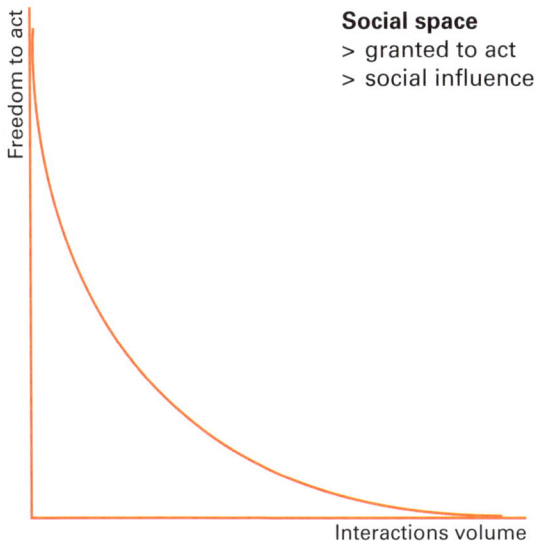

Social space
> granted to act
> social influence

Freedom to act

Interactions volume

Figure 26.
Social space:
success measured
by quantity of
interactions.

it is rewarded. The success of an organisation is shown to be related to the number of interactions it has with its environment, in a situation in which the organisation is more likely to adapt to the desires of that environment: more interactions mean more success, but also more dependence on the environment. This view would leave no room for the organisation's own ambitions. In other words, if the organisation is completely guided by the space offered by its social environment, it will develop in a reactive way and will therefore be of little value to that environment. An organisation that wants to create value must resist the 'mass inertia' of its environment in order to move it forward. It must create opportunities for itself to lead the way. There are three ways to do this: through improvement, through renewal, and through taking over the psychological space of the organisation itself (Figure 27).

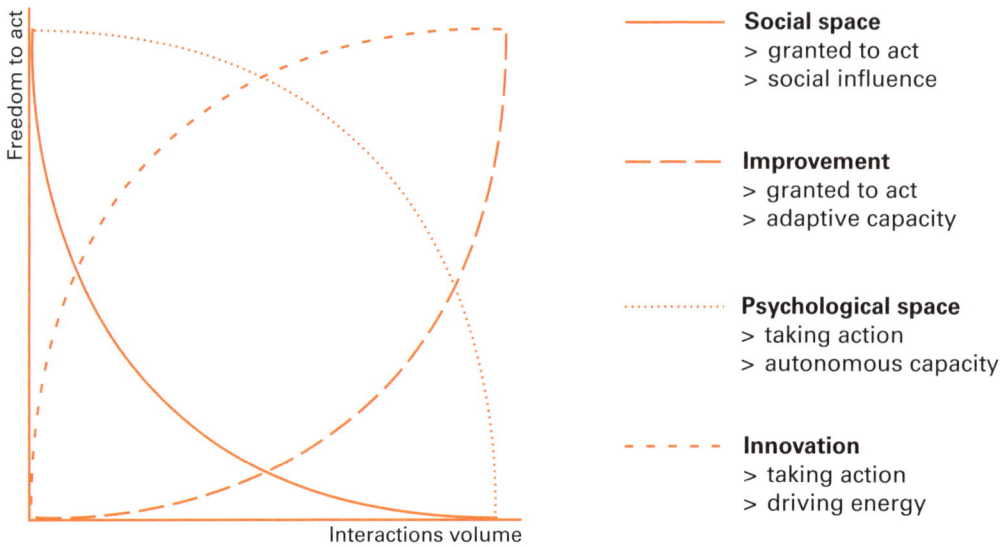

Figure 27.
Operating space
scenario's and
options: strategic
decisions based
on the perception
of the identity's
strength.

Social space
As described above, the success of the organisation acts as
an inhibiting factor here. The proposition is such that the
organisation has not really appropriated it, does not own it,
and is therefore dependent on public opinion. An example of
such a proposition can be found in the telecoms market, where
providers compete with each other to tailor their proposition as
much as possible to the consumer, and to make all sorts of offers
to make the choice attractive to that consumer. The key word
here is 'social influence': the pressure that the organisation feels
from outside.

Psychological space
This is the 180 degree version of social space: the organisation
feels strong enough to play an initiating role. Freedom of action
is not given but taken. In this category we find companies and
organisations that, on the basis of well-known propositions (in
most cases with little real innovative power), assume a leading

role simply by presenting themselves as leading. The market for fashionable items such as sports shoes is an example of this. We could also describe this variant as 'autonomous capacity', a concept that contains the danger of organisational autism. In essence, this is a purely marketing approach.

Improvement
In this option, the organisation proves itself to its environment. The response to the offer is used as a starting point for improving it, and the confidence gained as a result leads to more interaction with wider audiences. This is a scenario that occurs, for example, in the platform economy, where organisations work with learning processes based on minimum viable products and gradually grow towards a more accepted role through pivoting and perseverance. It is important for the organisation to have sufficient 'adaptive capacity' or resilience, not so much in a proactive sense as in a reactive sense.

Innovation
This is the most brutal of the four options, where organisations anticipate and even shape the environment, taking the freedom to develop something new and thereby gaining the trust of the environment. Here we find many developers of innovative products, often of a technological or scientific nature: from chip manufacturers to pharmaceuticals. These organisations are able to give energy to their environment, not only to their direct customers, but also to the market dynamics in which they find themselves. This is the 'Blue Ocean', as Kim and Mauborgne describe it.

The choice you make will, of course, depend on the origins and ambitions of your organisation. It must be appropriate and truthful. This requires awareness of your identity and acceptance of the consequences. In other words, the specific relationship of your identity between origin, development and responsibility. Then there is much to be gained. Gardena-Gröden was in danger of losing its connection with its immediate and vital environment by confining itself to its social space. Only when it dared to choose a strategy of renewal did it regain its value and its promise. Of course, the organisation of the Gardena-Gröden event involved a risk. That is why I said earlier that our real task was to restore the link between the world of sport and the valley community; if we had failed to do so, both the event and the community could have been seriously endangered. In other words, as strategists and designers, we are also responsible for the direction we take with our clients. (And as loyal pupils of Victor Papanek, we know only too well what that responsibility means). Again, identity turned out to be about connecting the dots. Telling the story of the valley and the event, and defining its identity in a tangible way, paved the way for renewal, visibility and connectivity. We choose, so we are.

The identity matrix
At the beginning of this chapter we saw the 'identity matrix' in its most original form. The basic idea behind the matrix can be found in the first chapter of this book: identity becomes visible in interaction with alterities. We need a counterpart, an environment, in order to be ourselves. The matrix describes this process in terms of outwardly directed themes, inwardly held values and the interactions between these themes and values.

Let's start with *themes:* these are the visible aspects of an identity, the things we see or suspect when we encounter an organisation. They are ordered so that they are more comprehensive from left to right. The 'motive' is what the organisation sees as its day-to-day business: this is on our desks every day, this is the common knowledge about us in our environment. It's what we do and what we're known for. We sell shoes. We provide tax advice. The 'goal' is what lies behind this day-to-day business: why we do it, what we achieve through our efforts, who we are important to at first glance. This is still something that the environment understands quite quickly.

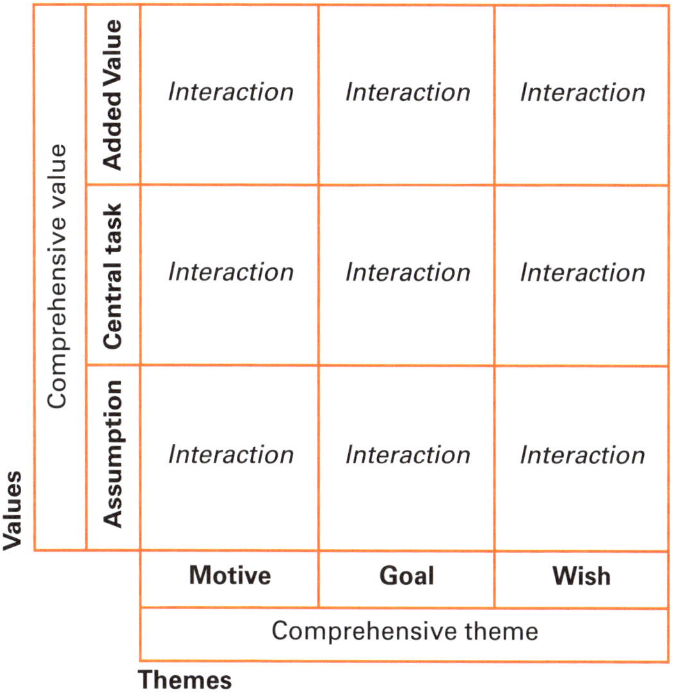

		Motive	Goal	Wish
Comprehensive value	**Added Value**	Interaction	Interaction	Interaction
	Central task	Interaction	Interaction	Interaction
	Assumption	Interaction	Interaction	Interaction
		Motive	**Goal**	**Wish**
		Comprehensive theme		

Values · Themes

Figure 28.
The 'identity matrix'.

We want to make a profit by selling shoes. We want to use our expertise in our services. The 'wish' is perhaps less obvious: this is the ambition of the organisation as a whole, not so much the goal of what it does, but where it wants to go in its actions. We want to be known for the quality of our shoes. We want to have a strong position in the consultancy market.

The *values,* on the other axis, describe what you might call the inner side or internal drivers of the organisation. They show what the organisation considers important. They show a similar progression to the themes, growing in importance from bottom to top. We start with the 'assumption': this is our starting point, the obvious value or belief without which we would not exist. The 'core purpose' describes what we consider to be our responsibility, the thing we work hard for, the reason we are committed to this organisation. And the 'value proposition' is what we want to offer the world in addition to what might be expected of us; what is it that ultimately makes us unique, outstanding, relevant and indispensable? What makes us tick, what do we celebrate about ourselves?

Confronting the 'external' issues with the 'internal' values then makes our identity visible. Again, identity is revealed in interaction with an alterity: how does the environment understand the organisation? To find these *interactions,* we link the values to the themes: what do we assume about our motive, goal and desire? What do we see as our central task for this motive, goal and desire? And how do we create added value for our motive, goal and desire?

Let's look again at the matrix of Gardena-Gröden. The themes describe the specific, visible character of the connection between the valley and the event: both are born in the nature that the valley offers, challenge is a central theme of our existence, fame is what makes us unique. This valley, with the specific challenges that its nature offers, is and wants to be famous — and everyone can see it. The values, our internal drivers, are closely linked to the cultural aspects of both the valley and the event: we value the fact that we are characteristic, we want to dedicate ourselves to who we are and who we want to be, and we are able to reach high levels in what we do. This valley is home to a capable community, because its inhabitants are dedicated to the specific characteristics of their environment.

Finding the interactions between themes and values is as creative a process as finding the themes and values themselves. It requires good conversations between knowledgeable people. When using the matrix, we set up quite large and diverse working groups to define the content of the identity matrix, because we need external and internal perspectives, experts and non-experts, directly involved and more distant stakeholders.

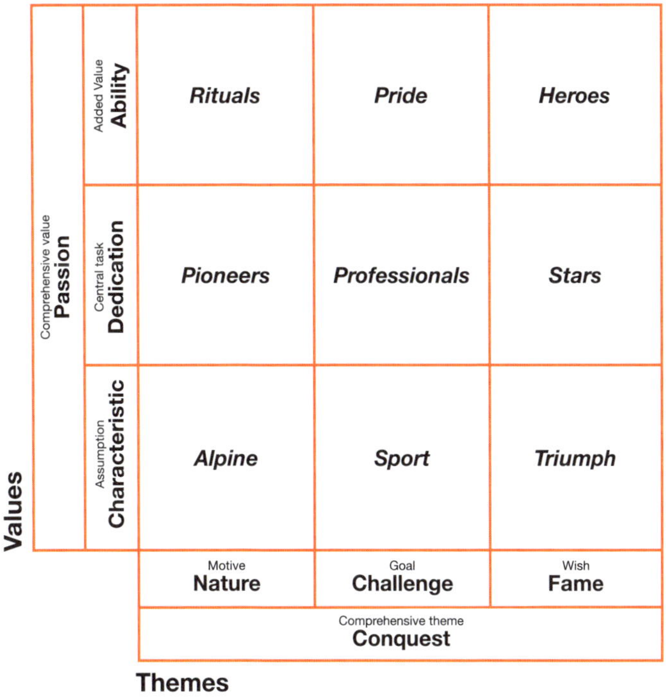

			Motive	Goal	Wish
		Ability Added Value	*Rituals*	*Pride*	*Heroes*
	Passion Comprehensive value	**Dedication** Central task	*Pioneers*	*Professionals*	*Stars*
		Characteristic Assumption	*Alpine*	*Sport*	*Triumph*

Values

Motive **Nature**	Goal **Challenge**	Wish **Fame**

Comprehensive theme
Conquest

Themes

Figure 29. Gardena-Gröden's 'identity matrix'.

The composition of the working group should, of course, reflect the interaction between the organisation and its environment.

In the Gardena-Gröden case, which deals with the relationship between valley and event, we found these interactions:

- **Characteristic for our Nature is that it is Alpine**
- **Characteristic for our Challenge is that it is about Sports**
- **Characteristic for the Fame we talk about is that it is about Triumph**
- **Our Dedication to our Nature made us Pioneers**
- **Our Dedication to our Challenge makes us Professionals**
- **Our Dedication to Fame creates Stars**
- **Our Ability in living in our Nature is visible in our Rituals**
- **Our Ability in meeting our Challenge creates Pride**
- **Our Ability in offering Fame creates Heroes**

Note that all these concepts are trying to describe the interaction between an inside and an outside, and between the valley and the event. Seen in this way, the matrix really became a description of the relationship between community and event, as all the concepts we found have this double meaning.

That's all very well, of course, but what can we do with this result? How have we used this identity matrix to develop the positioning, communication and corporate design of Val Gardena?

As I explained, the themes and values have a specific order, from the obvious to the more abstract, and from a smaller, everyday meaning to a more ambitious, transcendental one. In this way, the identity matrix shows what we call a "development dimension": if both the themes and the values show a development, the central development dimension is found in the central diagonal of the matrix.
In other words, this central diagonal shows the building blocks of the corporate story: where do we come from, what have we learned, what are our ambitions? You may have noticed that both the themes and the values have 'summaries' on the outer ring: thematically, the whole matrix is about 'conquest'; from a values perspective, it is about 'passion'. We have used these comprehensive versions to find the pay-off of Gardena-Gröden, simply by combining them: 'Passion for conquest'. Since we felt that this version was too one-sided and did not really value the efforts of both the valley community and the athletes, we adapted it to these efforts and ended up with 'Passion and Performance'.

When we started our original assignment, the corporate design and branding of Gardena-Gröden, we were now able to work with the matrix. If the themes are the visible part of the identity, we show them in symbols. And if the values are the more intangible parts of the identity, we express them in styles.

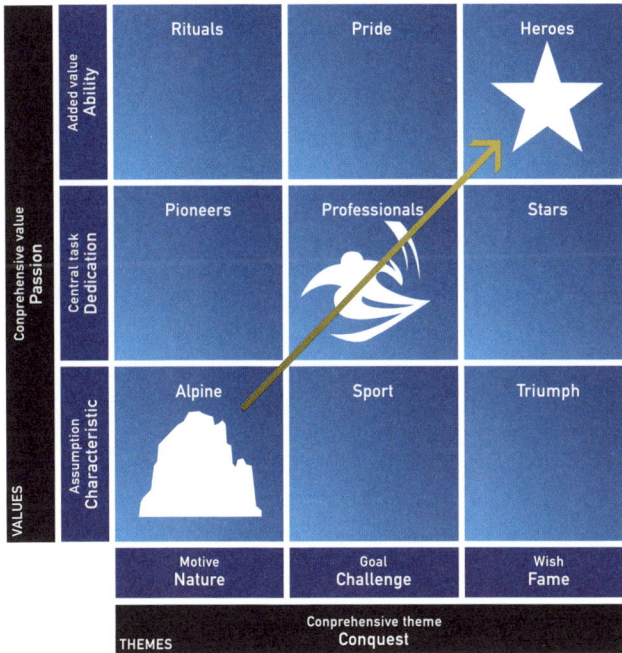

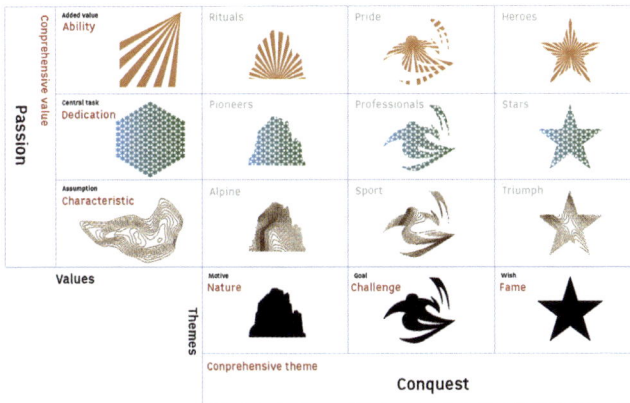

Gardena: creating alpine heroes through professionalism

Figure 30.
Top: Gardena-Gröden's identity matrix diagonal, representing its development direction. Bottom: translation of the identity matrix into visual elements.

We then considered that for the brand (the basic element of the corporate design) we should turn to the top right of the matrix: either we express that we are 'dedicated to challenge' or 'able to create fame'. As the world of alpine sports is highly competitive, and the community in the valley aspires to the highest standards, we chose the latter option. In the end, the matrix led us to create a brand that combines symbolism and style, pay-off, descriptor and the actual name of the event — and the valley that hosts it.

Passion and Performance

FIS Alpine Ski World Cup

GARDENA-GRÖDEN

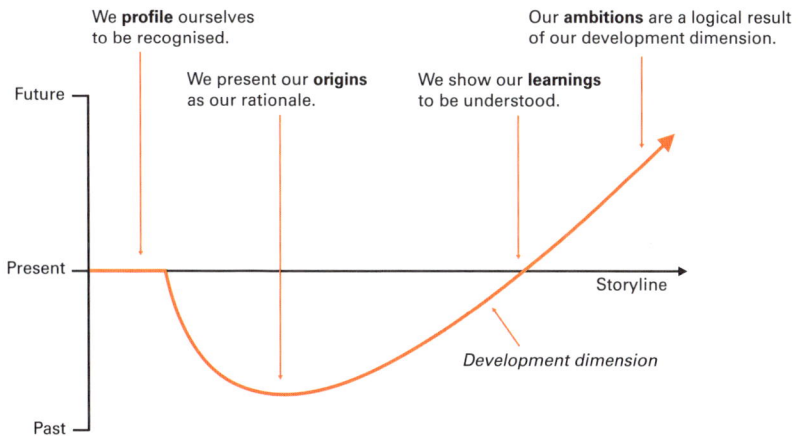

We **profile** ourselves
to be recognised.

We present our **origins**
as our rationale.

We show our **learnings**
to be understood.

Our **ambitions** are a logical result
of our development dimension.

Future

Present

Past

Storyline

Development dimension

Corporate story

Stories have a special talent for making the intangible tangible.
They can reflect not only what actually happened, but also what
lies behind what happened, the values, doubts, questions and
norms that gave way to those events. They create a reality that
is not only more complete, but also more comprehensible to us
as human beings. I think the shortest definition of a corporate
story is that it links origins, learning and future in such a way
that it conveys the beliefs, challenges and ambitions of the
organisation. That's quite a mouthful, so let's break it down.

Note 14.
Edsco de Heus
and Dmitri
Berkhout created
their version of
this model in their
2009 essay.

Figure 31.
Corporate story
modelled as a
representation of
the organisation's
development.

Two of my former colleagues summarised their thoughts on the
corporate story in a model that I have slightly adapted here.[14]
This diagram shows the relationship between the timeline
of the story and that of the organisation. First we recognise
the organisation, then we tell the story of how it became the
organisation we know, which we then recognise and understand
as the basis for its ambition: this is why we are here and why
we want to go there. It again describes the relationship between
origins, development and responsibility: we have built on our

origins in a particular direction, our development dimension, and we will continue to do so. And in doing so, we take responsibility for who we are, because we will remain true to ourselves. But there's more. You don't write a corporate story for nothing. It is aimed at a wide range of audiences, both internal and external, both near and far. It aims to inspire, persuade, connect and engage. It has the unique power to do all these things at once — provided it leaves some room for interpretation by those audiences. In other words, it should be written in such a way that it connects the reality of the organisation with the reality of the target groups. It needs empathy.

Corporate stories can take any form — as long as they contain the elements shown above. I have written corporate stories as short as two paragraphs and as long as 10 chapters. Some used technical language, others were more metaphorical. The corporate story of Maasstad Hospital in Rotterdam focused on the interaction between the hospital and its immediate environment. And when I wrote the corporate story of the National Museum of Literature, I couldn't resist the temptation to write a novel… Anything that can create a link between the organisation and its target groups: customers, employees, stakeholders, shareholders is allowed. At the same time, I have learned to restrain myself. The story should be true, honest and trustworthy. We don't polish up our organisation, but show it as it is, authentically, honestly and to the point.

The Gardena-Gröden story was written by Manuel Demetz and Gernot Mussner and took a journalist's view of the event and its origins. It describes the big idea and the small details, the humble beginnings and the big ambitions, the valley community and the sports world, the people and their challenges, the difficult times and the successes. Ultimately, it is a story of heroes: overcoming challenges by pioneering and innovating in a way that is true to ourselves. Because that is what Gardena-Gröden does: it can make everybody a hero.

Figure 32.
Südtiroler Wirtschaftszeitung, september 28, 2007.

---

20 ·· **Firmennachrichten** — Südtiroler Wirtschaftszeitung · No. 37 | 07 – Freitag, 28. September 2007

Export – Tanzer Maschinenbau in Lana wickelt in diesen Tagen einen besonderen Auftrag ab

Ruf aus Los Angeles

Eine (patentierte) überdimensionale Zentrifuge für Mehrweg-Kunststoffkisten liefert Tanzer Maschinenbau in diesen Tagen nach Los Angeles. Das Unternehmen bezeichnet sich als Prototypenbauer – **ist aber viel mehr.**

Peter Tanzer (rechts) und Projektleiter Matthias Gufler mit der Zentrifuge

Tourismus – „Historische" Auszeichnung für Parkhotel Holzner

Krönung

Das Parkhotel Holzner in Oberbozen am Ritten ist der „Historische Gastbetrieb des Jahres in Südtirol". **Wie die Jury das begründet.**

Marianne und Hans Holzner bei der Preisverleihung

Corporate Identity – Neue Marke für Grödner Ski-Höhepunkt

Weltcupstern

Der Grödner Ski-Weltcup hat ein neues Corporate Design. **Es stammt aus den Niederlanden**, hat aber auch Grödner „Blut".

Passion and Performance
FIS Alpine Ski World Cup
GARDENA-GRÖDEN

Kälte-Klima-Röhler – Firmengebäude in Bozen-Süd im Beisein vieler Gäste eröffnet

Der neue KKR-Sitz

Mit einer dem Unternehmen angemessenen „coolen" Feier hat die in der Klimabranche tätige KKR GmbH ihren **neuen Sitz in Bozen-Süd** offiziell eröffnet – mit Gästen und Mitarbeitern.

Die Unternehmerfamilie Röhler mit Gästen (v.l.): Klaus Röhler, Peter Röhler Schwetzer, Heidi Röhler, Peter Röhler, Hansi Röhler, Herbert Fritz

By establishing ourselves, we take responsibility for what we have created.

We stay true to ourselves
by reflecting on our origins,
development and responsibility.

We involve diverse stakeholders and organise our own counter-power in defining who we are.

We are the stewards of our story.

Development and innovation

The development of an organisation requires a deep understanding of the significance of its origins and of the value of its dialogue with the environment. The organisation needs to stay in touch with itself in order to slowly carve its image from the rough marble. Growth is a process of reflection and interaction, focused on one's own origins.
However, this dialogue with itself and its environment cannot be free. In order to create the dynamics necessary for self-fulfilment, risks must be taken here and there. We assume legitimacy because the organisation exists — but its relevance must be proven and its existence must be granted time and again. In this way, innovation is not so much a process of inventing as of constantly recreating yourself.
The organisation has a role to play that emerges over time; whether it is understood and embraced depends on the degree of awareness of one's own role and the real courage to accept challenges and to stand by one's role and responsibility.
Identity facilitates not only innovation, but ultimately identity itself. Identity is renewal history.

Identity as a touchpoint for the environment.

Positioning and marketing your organisation.

Maester shows how to develop a collaboration driven platform.

The 'positioning triangle' and the 'marketing matrix'.

5

Collaboration.

Identity can connect you.

Maester.
How knowledge sharing made everybody grow.

Knowledge management is a particular challenge for many organisations. We live and work in a highly knowledge-based economy and society in which we are constantly in danger of falling behind. At the same time, organisations have a core purpose, and apart from actual knowledge, research and (technological) innovation institutions and companies, knowledge tends not to be it. It is a vital, but usually conditional, aspect of the management and development of an organisation or a sector. Having the right knowledge at the right time, in the right people and stakeholders, with the right maturity and appropriation, can give you a significant advantage, whether in a competitive environment or in the public and political sphere. Or, to put it the other way round, not having any of this is a big risk.

At the risk of kicking down an open door, speed is of the essence. Getting the knowledge you need to do your job, but too late; or not getting it fast enough to the people or stakeholders who need it to make the right decisions or develop initiatives or innovations — are the same problems as not having the knowledge at all. The challenge is to be alert to relevant developments, to identify which knowledge is critical, to prioritise the most important issues, to select the right sources, and to have an ongoing process for actually acquiring and managing the knowledge itself — all in a timely manner and with sufficient checks and balances. Many organisations have processes and procedures, and sometimes even dedicated managers and staff, to do all this — but this requires investment that not every organisation or sector is able or willing to make.

One of the challenges of knowledge management is sourcing. Where do you find the knowledge you need, and how reliable is it? If you are going to base your decisions, strategic or otherwise, on the information you have, you need to be very sure of it. Using multiple sources, peer communication, consultants and experienced analysts, and of course your own people who should be experts in their field, is the way to go — but again, this all takes time and not every organisation has the luxury (in time or resources) to go there.

There is also the issue of the sensitivity of knowledge in a competitive environment. In many cases, you do not want to share too much of what you know, because the competition (or your political opponents, for example) can easily deduce what you do and do not know — and then use your knowledge or lack of it against you. At the same time, you need to assess your knowledge position, and discussion with others is one of the best ways to do this.
The good news is that not all the knowledge you need is confidential information. There is a lot of knowledge that is vital to any organisation that does not need to be 'kept secret'. For example, in the public sector, such as in healthcare or education, we expect high quality services at the lowest possible cost. After all, this is public money that needs to be spent on the core purposes of the organisations and sectors in this area. Non-competitive knowledge on issues such as hygiene or safety management is just as important as more competitive knowledge — but it has to be built up by each individual organisation, investing time and money.

A final challenge in all of this is that much of the knowledge is in the people. And employees, however loyal, do not stay forever. Especially in the more knowledge-based sectors, there is a high turnover of employees. People can change jobs, leave for various reasons, or retire (which means they leave just when they are the most experienced people you have). And when they leave, their knowledge goes with them. They may even take it to the competition. Again, many organisations have processes and procedures in place to protect their knowledge position. They may have central databases of direct knowledge, best practices and cases, use a student mentor structure to transfer knowledge from senior to junior staff, and have all sorts of training benefits in place. But even if you can afford to do all this, the effort is intense and takes up perhaps a disproportionate amount of your time and resources.

An essential aspect of running an organisation that often has limited resources to allocate to that same aspect — this is the situation that inspired Haarlem-based start-up Maester to think about a different approach to knowledge sharing. The idea was simple: if the same knowledge is built up and made available in many organisations, it is not very efficient. So why not share knowledge on a give-and-take basis? What if we could make a deal to share knowledge between organisations, where each would 'pay' with the knowledge they have in exchange for the knowledge the other organisation has? Of course, we can see many obstacles to this idea: the sensitivity of information and knowledge, especially in a competitive environment; the effort it would take to organise the exchange of knowledge as such; the differences between organisations in terms of the needs and specifications of the knowledge, ... But still, the idea is very elegant. The question is not why, but how to do it, thought Maester.

The 'how' turned out to be the development of a SaaS platform for learning. This simple sentence shows a lot of ingenuity on Maester's part. First of all, building a platform for knowledge sharing is a different way of thinking than, for example, creating a central database, setting up knowledge training or programming a lecture series. It means making available something that already exists somewhere, but has been inaccessible. In this case: Maester provides access to knowledge that does not belong to them, but to the participants of the platform. Knowledge that is used by its owner on a daily basis stays where it is, is constantly updated and is therefore a trusted source.
Second, building relationships on a SaaS basis makes those relationships both interactive and long-term. A SaaS exchange

platform requires commitment from all parties. Its value grows in both volume and time, and the commitment to that relationship is supported by the SaaS structure, where you pay per participant and at the level of that commitment. However, it is the third aspect of the above sentence that I find most appealing: Maester is not talking about knowledge, it is talking about learning. That is, they are talking about knowledge in action, in its dynamic and meaningful form. A learning exchange platform constantly builds knowledge and, by its very nature, ensures that this knowledge is acquired by the people who need it. Now think about some of the challenges we mentioned above: speed, trust and acquisition by the relevant employees — all solved by a single approach.

One aspect of Maester's success is that the tool they provide needs to be complemented by a community of users. Only in this way can Maester ensure that the knowledge presented through the platform is relevant, up-to-date and trustworthy. Thinking and acting like a community will ensure that common interests remain at the heart of everything that is presented or developed. Maester therefore had to invest not only in technological development and the creation of an access structure, but also in building this community. In addition to Software as a Service, they also offered Community as a Service.

Two interrelated paths were followed. Maester distinguished between users (larger groups of employees who only use the platform to learn themselves) and corporate product owners (people working in the client organisations who are responsible for learning and development). It started to organise community meetings on the Maester platform with these product owners, where relationships between the participants were established, relevant topics and content were discussed, but also the functioning and content management of the platform itself was a topic. Involving the participants in the development of not only the content but also the platform itself proved to be an important, if not essential, channel for the development of both the community and the platform. Importantly, these community meetings are facilitated by the platform itself: all communication between all parties involved takes place through the Maester platform, making it a single source of truth for both content and meta-information.

But the core of Maester's and the community's success was the second way of building the knowledge community: its content strategy. The platform facilitates not only the study of content, but also its adaptation and enrichment. Maester's content takes the form of trainings and courses (after all, this is about learning), which can be studied and used by all participants. In addition, each user can (with some moderation built into the platform) adapt these trainings and courses to the specific needs of their own organisation, or enrich them with knowledge — and then post them back to the platform.

How does it work? Let's say there is a hospital that has placed its hygiene management training on the Maester platform. Someone from another hospital, responsible for training, looks for such a course and finds it on Maester, but discovers that there are some differences in quality assurance or that something seems outdated. He adapts and enriches the training, puts it back on the platform as content provided by his hospital and, after some moderation by Maester's experts, makes it available to any other user of the platform.[15]

This collaborative effort to continuously improve the content not only ensures the relevance and trustworthiness of up-to-date content, but also contributes greatly to the sense of community on the platform. Just by using the Maester platform, users get to know each other and the expertise that exists in other organisations. The only real challenge here was the nature of the knowledge: anything of competitive

Note 15.
This is a description of the situation of around 2020, when we were working with Maester. Since then, this process has been largely automated, among other things through the implementation of AI. Moreover, the platform now also offers to build complete trainings and training programmes from scratch, through automation, embedded expertise and AI and using the content of the platform for mining. In other words, apart from the user-provided content, also new generation of content based on the existing content is now made possible by the Maester platform.

value is, for obvious reasons, limited in its ability to be shared. The solution here was to reverse this: Maester targets non-competitive, often secondary process knowledge, and sectors with mandates that require efficient sourcing: the public sector, not-for-profits and NGOs. Maester realised that it needed to target sectors, i.e. knowledge sharing between organisations with similar missions and responsibilities. Think of healthcare, water boards, education or governments at local or regional level. Maester is a semi-open platform where anyone can connect and engage, not only to gain knowledge but also to add value. This gives the platform a socially engaged character.[16]

Maester started in 2014 and after about 5 years encountered the typical problem of a scale-up: the need to grow, but the lack of resources to do so. It needed financial, expertise and management resources to take the next step. This is where Creative Capital Studio came in, where I was a venture partner at the time. Creative Capital Studio is a group of seasoned, highly experienced experts in various fields such as strategy, product development, marketing, recruitment, legal and finance. This group invests and acts in soft tech scale-ups — but in a special way. In addition to financial resources, they also bring hands-on expertise: the partners and venture Partners temporarily 'add' themselves to the investee company and act as experienced employees. During their involvement, they accelerate whatever is needed to make the next stage of scale-up a reality — and then leave. Reimbursement is in the form of a share in the scale-up, as with any other investment company.

In the case of Maester, we felt it was necessary to support the company in its product development, strategy, marketing and branding, as well as its legal and financial processes, and we provided the necessary experts to do so. We supported Maester in two phases: a defining phase in which we worked with Maester to discover what this was all about, where it could go and what 'pivot' might be necessary, and a creative phase

Note 16.
To a limited extent, Maester is also used in a closed variant by larger companies as an internal learning facility.

in which we developed and activated the means to actually follow the defined path. My role was to develop the strategic marketing and support the branding of Maester.

The first step was to find the core of the company: what was the compelling, inspiring and guiding story behind it all? How did the founder's original idea evolve into the current proposition of a SaaS-based e-learning environment? What made Maester a special player? To whom was this proposition relevant or, conversely, in which markets and situations could it be promising to enter and build relationships?

In an organically iterative and interactive process, we found a very strong pay-off in the short phrase 'Leren van elkaar' ('Learning from each other'). It looks simple, but it's not. The pay-off describes both Maester's core proposition (knowledge management through learning and sharing knowledge between people and organisations) and the conduct principle for the whole of Maester. We found that this principle also drove product development (e.g. 'Will this proposed direction of the product strengthen learning from each other?'), corporate culture and labour market communications (e.g. 'We are looking for employees who want to develop themselves by learning from each other and giving others the opportunity to do so.'), marketing (e.g. 'In which sectors is it possible to exchange knowledge — where can we find circumstances that facilitate learning from each other?') and branding (e.g. 'We are a co-creative community where members learn from each other.)

In terms of strategic marketing, we started with the same idea: if Maester is about learning, so should our marketing. We defined a marketing strategy based on organic growth: step by step, logical and thorough growth, taking into account that the quality of the knowledge and the platform are key and should never be compromised. After all, we are talking about a trustworthy source of knowledge. To achieve this growth, we

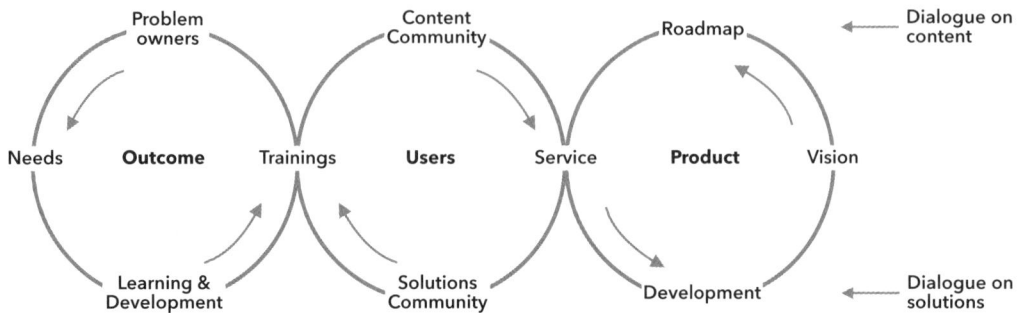

have followed what we call the 'adjacent markets' principle: once we have established ourselves and gained experience in a particular market, we look for a comparable or 'neighbouring' market to expand into. In other words, our market development must be organic and content-based: we must already have a content proposition to conquer the new market. So we expanded from local government to water boards because they have similar challenges and solutions, used our content on hygiene in healthcare to enter other markets where hygiene is an issue, and so on.

Maester offers many benefits to its clients. In the proposition text we described it as 'Maester provides a space for creating, sharing and finding knowledge in the form of training courses focused on specific, socially driven sectors; offers advice on formatting knowledge in the form of training and encourages knowledge sharing and development through community building; and offers managed services on an accessible platform, training formats and sharing tools, and additional communication tools for interaction regarding the content on the platform'.
But we have also described it in other ways, since the product is not only a SaaS. Maester acts as the driving force and facilitator of the topic and content-driven communities it hosts, offering a 'Community as a Service'. As a strong supporter of educational culture and an important factor in the attractiveness of its

Figure 33.
The internal learning cycles of Maester.

Targets 2021				
SALES	PMC1 water boards PMC0 core community	PMC2 municipalities PMC1 water boards PMC0 core community	PMC3 health care PMC2 municipalities PMC1 water boards PMC0 core community	PMC4 tbd PMC3 health care PMC2 municipalities PMC1 water boards PMC0 core community

CORPORATE	Positioning and profiling:
	  familiarity
	Corporate content: share
		Positioning and profiling:
		  maintenance
		Corporate content:
		  familiarity
		Monitoring and PR:
		  development
			Positioning and profiling:
			  maintenance
			Corporate content:
			  maintenance
			Monitoring and PR:
			  adjustments
				Positioning and profiling:
				  maintenance
				Corporate content:
				  maintenance
				Monitoring and PR:
				  adjustments

LABOUR MARKET	EVP: familiarity Jobs content: share	EVP: familiarity Jobs content: maintenance	EVP: familiarity Jobs content: maintenance	EVP: familiarity Jobs content: maintenance
	Q1	**Q2**	**Q3**	**Q4**

Figure 34.
Maester's market growth model.

customers' workplaces. As a facilitator of non-core tasks, as a means of personalising learning in the context of an organisation, as a revenue model for sharing knowledge (which was eventually translated into the Maester currency of 'Maester Participation Units' or MPU's).

In positioning and branding all these aspects, we focused on the simple fact that when we learn with Maester, we learn from each other; so connecting with Maester means connecting with each other. Connection, community building and participation became the key ideas for positioning. And inclusivity and commitment, translated into the lemma 'Be a Maester', its communicative summary.

Next, we used a model that I developed myself to order and design the marketing strategy. I will explain the model in more detail later, but for now I will just say that it is a matrix that links the development process of marketing as such with the path from positioning to branding. In other words, the two axes describe the necessary development in terms of process and content, with which the matrix represents a roadmap for marketing.

	Positioning	Thought leadership	Communication	Branding
Think	Central statement 'Leren van elkaar': co-creative training and learning	Relevant issues, themes and markets Facilitating non-core tasks Knowledge sharing Learning community	Communication strategy Content in stead of benefits Dominantly through the platform itself	Brand strategy Monolithic and consistent on high quality and trustworthiness
Create	Message house Pay-off, boilerplate, one-pager, Q&A	Content Elaboration on the themes	Communication building blocks Content descriptions and basic statements, owned channel development	Brand building blocks New visual identity, boldness, consistent attentive behaviour
Activate	PR and PA Near markets: similar issues and themes and adjacent markets	Publishing Blogging, knowledge events, lectures, online community	Means, media and channels Owned channels, market dominant media, knowledge platforms	Campaigning Online in knowledge relevant fora
Prove	Participation level Monitoring engagement, response and growth	Visible dialogue Visibility of themes and insights in our markets	Monitoring (share and domain) On own platform and through third party tools	Monitoring (recognition, NPS) On own platform and through user surveys

The top two lines were partly filled in by summarising what we had found in the strategy definition and in the search for the key customer and his journey. Some parts had to be built from scratch, such as the communications strategy. And the bottom two lines were filled in in a second phase of the collaboration between Maester and Creative Capital Studio, where we worked on the translation and implementation of the marketing through sales, content creation et cetera. These parts were complemented by discussions with the Maester team, looking at the habits, channels, tools and media that were known and dominant in the sectors that Maester were addressing at the time. We used what was already there and added what was missing for Maester's objectives. Maester then used this tool to harmonise their marketing efforts and activate the results we had achieved in the earlier process. From then on, they were able to act autonomously in their marketing efforts.Identity aspects.

Figure 35.
Maester's marketing matrix.

Identity aspects

I have had many discussions with clients about the power of identity. Most clients see the power of their identity as the ability to make themselves visible, distinct, special. They assume that successful positioning in the marketplace requires a distinctive brand. In most cases I disagree. In my experience, it is not distinctiveness that gives you a position in your environment, but your connectedness.

First of all, in many cases there is confusion about the definition of a corporate identity on the one hand and a brand on the other. I don't want to get too deep into this discussion here (and I'll come back to 'branding' later in this section), but for now let's say that I define a brand as something that is built by your target audiences — helped by specific, dedicated efforts on your part. Brands are psychological constructs, brain locations, in the minds and sometimes hearts of your target audiences. You may launch a brand and manage its success, but its meaning is not yours, it is your audience's.

Your identity, on the other hand, as you may have understood by now, is not what people understand about you, but your own intrinsic personality. It is the very essence of who you are. And it only becomes visible in the interaction between you and your environment. That is, in the connections you make. If brands are about distinctiveness, identities are about connectivity. They do not aim for visibility, as brands do (in fact, they do not aim for anything, as I said earlier), but they make you relevant, which is something quite different.

Being relevant means that you play a role in people's considerations as a value that they subscribe to, as something or someone that is of real importance to them, to whom they can connect, in short, on the basis of mutual recognition, not on the basis of a sender-receiver relationship. Dialogue and interaction are central and essential. And for that you need relevant content and mutual understanding. In Maester's case, this was exactly the core of the approach: relevance and connection are the basic tools of positioning and marketing strategy, since the content provided and its relevance are at the heart of the proposition. (In the next chapter, I will return to making connections with your audiences and the power of relevance).

The fact that Maester is a platform makes specific demands on its positioning and marketing. Platforms obviously do not own their content, but merely facilitate its exchange. Their own identity therefore develops on a meta-level: the selection and management of content makes clear what the platform is about. Airbnb is about private home rentals, Booking is about hotels, X is about sharing opinions. The challenge is to keep your identity independent of what is offered on the platform, while at the same time guaranteeing the quality of that content — and of your facilitation, of course. You can do this by appropriating themes derived from the content you offer. Airbnb uses the character of your stay as a theme: is it a holiday, a city trip, a hike in the mountains? Are you a family, a group of friends, alone? And so on. If you want to position yourself successfully in a particular market, these themes and your management of them should be better than your competitors' efforts. You need to achieve thought leadership in your content.

Maester did this by analysing its own relevance to customers and identifying themes such as 'non-core tasks of the organisation' and 'personalised learning in an organisational context'. Continually focusing on these topics will give you an advantage as you become a thought leader on them over time. Your market share will grow because you make a clear choice of what you consider to be your market. From there, you can grow organically into other markets and topics, just as Maester does with his 'adjacent markets' strategy.

You may remember what we talked about in the first chapter of this book: the vital connection between identity and interaction.

Identities are only fulfilled when they are perceived by another identity (an 'alterity'); at the same time, they necessarily point to themselves: they show their own character and values through this perception. I like to see this phenomenon as the natural playground and fulfilment of identity: since identity is not static, but a dynamic, resilient and constantly evolving asset of the organisation, it needs this interaction to have this dynamic character. I don't mean here what is usually called the "learning organisation" (in my opinion this term refers to the operational character and sometimes the strategy of an organisation), but something more essential: the organisation as such, which evolves over time. It needs a context to change and grow. It needs a counter-force from the environment, a 'mould' as we called it in Chapter 1 — but this mould also turns out to be dynamic. Organisations become resilient when they are able to remain open to their environment and respond in an authentic way, true to their character and values — in short, when they are trustworthy.

For Maester, of course, trustworthiness is a critical success factor. If you are going to rely on the content offered by such a platform, you need to be sure (and convinced) of its quality. Maester has solved this problem by focusing on shared knowledge, offering its clients the knowledge of peer organisations with similar challenges. Because such decisions are made 'out in the open', they may appear opportunistic or simply a response to the market as such: 'we see an opportunity here'; but, as you will have understood, I see it as more essential.

Organisations can sometimes seem opportunistic. They show their interests and visibly try to influence their context, and we don't always accept that. (Of course, we could also say that organisations may be more honest than individuals). The response of most organisations to criticism like this is to bombard it with communications. Over and over again, objectives are explained and ambitions defended. The effect is completely counterproductive. Not only because of what is said, because of the defensive nature of what is being communicated, because of the often over-convincing tone, but also simply because it is being said.

Organisations need to recognise that in the 21st century, people are inundated with information, with persuasion, with the ambitions of others. We no longer see the information forest for all the message trees. And an organisation that keeps trying to get its message across will at best cut an open space in that forest and call that space its domain or its purpose. And then — we lose trust. We see this too often. At the same time, any action that is authentic, that is in line with the natural response of the organisation's identity to developments in the environment, does not need to be explained. If the environment does not immediately understand, patience and perseverance will eventually make it clear why the organisation is developing in a certain direction: because it is its natural direction. In other words, it is simply following its corporate story.

Once launched, Maester faced the same challenge: the new company entered the open playground of identity, where it had to interact with the environment to become visible and relevant. The particular challenge here was to do this in such a way that this environment would trust the new organisation, since trust is essential for success in the knowledge market. (Of course, trust is essential for any organisation, for building and maintaining good relationships). We developed a strong trust proposition through relevant content, through careful selection of topics, but above all: by making listening to customers an integral part of the proposition. Product owners discuss not only the content, but also the facilities that Maester offers them — and this is reflected in the product development of the platform.
This approach is important. Showing what you understand, how alert you are and how you respond to your clients' challenges makes you someone to be taken very seriously; and developing

that knowledge openly with anyone who is interested gives you authority: you can obviously afford to share all this because you are already taking the next step in your thinking.

This is exactly what a thought leader is: an organisation that can open itself up to the world, that is not afraid to debate and perhaps lose debates, that holds opinions that may be challenged but are backed up by deep knowledge and innovative insights. A thought leader has a natural leadership position in the marketplace and can — or more importantly, is expected to — demonstrate its character. A thought leader claims territory and has authority in that territory. Thought leaders are the best-positioned organisations there are, because the market has expectations of them; their opinions and insights are expected.

In strategic marketing, thought leadership is therefore essential. It validates the organisation's position, adds credibility to the brand and consistency to the organisation's narrative. It makes the relevance of the organisation to a certain domain very clear. And it answers questions before they are asked. For the identity of any organisation, achieving thought leadership is a solid engine for its development and visibility, as it forces the organisation to reflect on its direct and indirect environment, as well as itself, and thus create its own 'mould' for interaction.

In the previous chapter we talked about the ethical dimension of identity, which I described as the responsibility for what one has created in establishing oneself. In the case of Maester, we find a social aspect in the choice of markets and themes: Maester facilitates the efficiency of knowledge management for organisations in the public domain, i.e. it contributes to a better allocation of the resources of these organisations. In turn, Maester has the responsibility to continue doing this and to develop more tools for efficient knowledge management. The simple but very effective approach is to make this responsibility part of the proposition: Maester offers more possibilities with every development, learning from its customers what the missing links are and how to prioritise them. Here we see a clear example of the 'reciprocity' of identity: its value goes hand in hand with the value it creates for others.

Beyond the platform itself, we saw in the case description that Maester also needed to develop and facilitate a community of users and product owners. Only then could the proposition of 'learning from each other' be realised. Building and managing such a community requires specific efforts: facilities for its communication and coherence, of course; topics and questions to be discussed; a definition of the conditions under which people can participate in discussions; and so on. Again, identity plays a role. Communities are maintained by their members (not by their facilitators) and therefore develop a certain character autonomously. This autonomy is important. If the facilitator becomes too involved in the direction of the community, it ceases to be a community.

Communities need to create a culture of trust, sharing, reciprocity and value. Nurturing this culture is all the facilitator can do; and one of the tools is to recognise its identity and make it clear to everyone. In order not to disrupt the community process and to protect its autonomy, this requires a very careful approach, with small triggers at the right moments to show what is happening, what the community is becoming and what this means for its initiatives and development.

Maester's conduct principle 'Leren van elkaar' (learning from each other) once again proved its worth. It establishes a culture of mutuality and trust without questioning it, as it describes the very core and meaning of the community. The fact that the Maester itself is one of the 'learners' points to the authenticity of the claim. And it serves as a decision-making principle at all times when community members discuss either the content or the development of the Maester platform itself.

To conclude this section, a final comment on the fascinating subject of brands. As I tried to explain earlier, brands are curiously of limited relevance to identities. If identity is about character, values and authenticity, brands are about recognisability, appeal and consistency. They have a different role to play. Identities grow in the same way a personality does: through confrontation, insight, setbacks, epiphanies and reflection; they grow themselves. Brands do not grow; their perception does. I believe that a strong brand is born of the fact that it does not explain itself. It should be the target group's discovery of what the brand stands for — because then the brand gets a place in the brain. It gets attention. A brand is not a storyteller, but a provocateur of stories. Brands grow in ascribed meaning, in the minds of the target group, and the more mysterious they are, the more exciting they can become, the greater this growth will be. This is also why well-designed brands explain nothing; the public has to understand where this behaviour, shape and style come from — and while they are trying to do that, the brand already has a brain position that can then be reinforced by consistent branding: behaviour, product and service development, positions and presentation of the organisation behind the brand.

This approach to branding has led me to the marketing roadmap model I presented in the case study and which I will describe in more detail later in this chapter. But first, let's look at the relationship between identity and positioning in our increasingly interactive environment.

Modelling for positioning
In their famous book *The Discipline of Market Leaders*, Michael Treacy and Fred Wiersema make one thing clear: to position yourself, you have to choose — and then stick to your choice. The book is full of examples of companies that have made bold, unexpected and adverse choices, stuck with them and thrived. Why is that? Because making tough, bold choices and sticking

'best product'
Product Leadership

Product differentiation

Operational competence

Customer responsive

Operational Excellence
'best total cost'

Customer Intimacy
'best total solution'

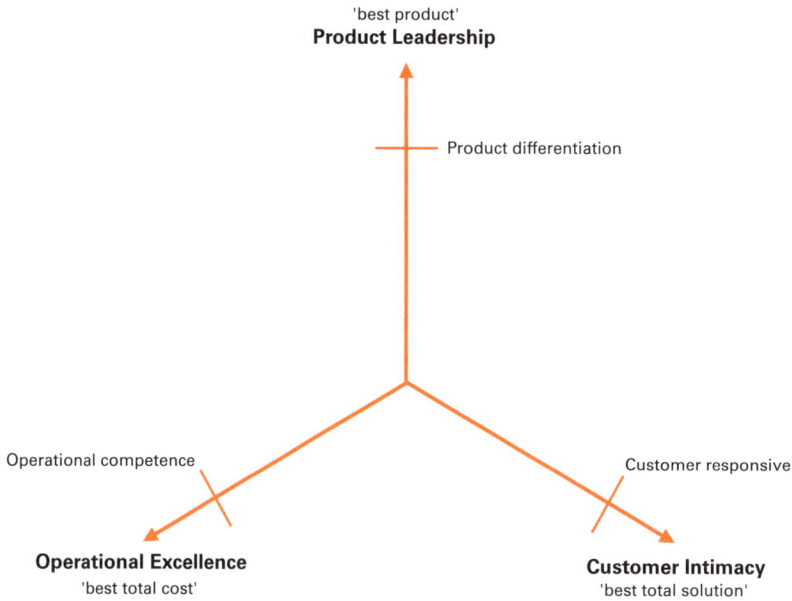

to them makes you very visible. It gives you a position. In some ways this is similar to what Kim and Mauborgne later describe in their Blue Ocean strategy, but Treacy and Wiersema manage to distil the idea of choice into a now world famous decision model for positioning (Figure 36).

The first message here, of course, is that you have to choose. You cannot sit in the middle, at the risk of being invisible and incomprehensible: what are you really about? Treacy and Wiersema believe that there are only three choices: either you go for cost leadership (not the cheapest, perhaps, but the best value for money), which they call 'operational excellence', because it depends on how well you manage to organise yourself and your processes; or you go for the best product (which could also be a service, of course) and aim for top quality rather than the best value for money — this is called 'product leadership'; or you position yourself for the most comprehensive approach

Figure 36.
Treacy and Wiersema's threshold and leadership model.

and deliver the best total solution for the customer, a top-of-the-range product made to measure and priced accordingly — this is called 'customer intimacy'.

The corresponding efforts or qualities of your organisation also become clear: for operational excellence, you obviously need operational competence; for product leadership, you need a sophisticated product or product differentiation capabilities; and for customer intimacy, you need customer responsiveness. In other words, which position you choose depends on what you already are or what is close to you and can be developed or enhanced. The model makes you choose something that is or comes close to your identity.

There's a lot more to be said about this model (and Treacy and Wiersema do, of course), such as the importance of thresholds (can you deliver in a credible, distinctive or even unique way?), but I want to go in one particular direction: the way an organisation can use the model to link its identity to the market 'out there' and turn that into a mission 'in here', as I described in Chapter 3. How do you 'live' your positioning? How do you become who you say you are?

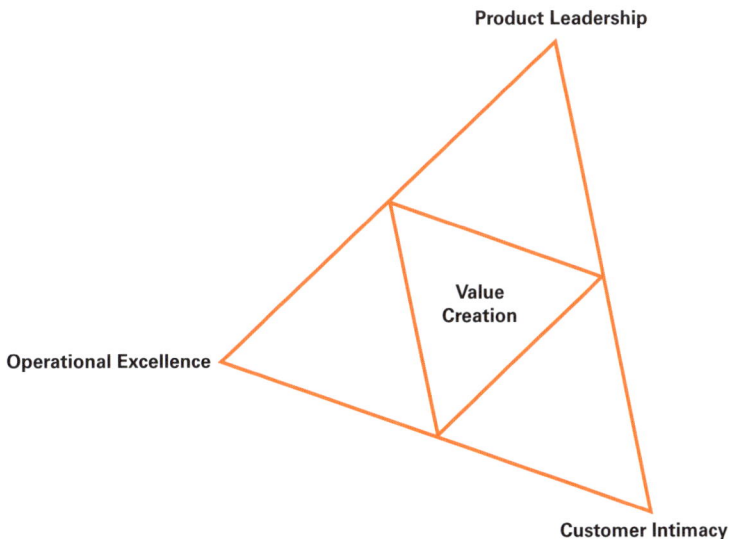

Figure 37.
My preferred representation of Treacy and Wiersema's thought on leadership.

Product Leadership

Value Creation

Operational Excellence

Customer Intimacy

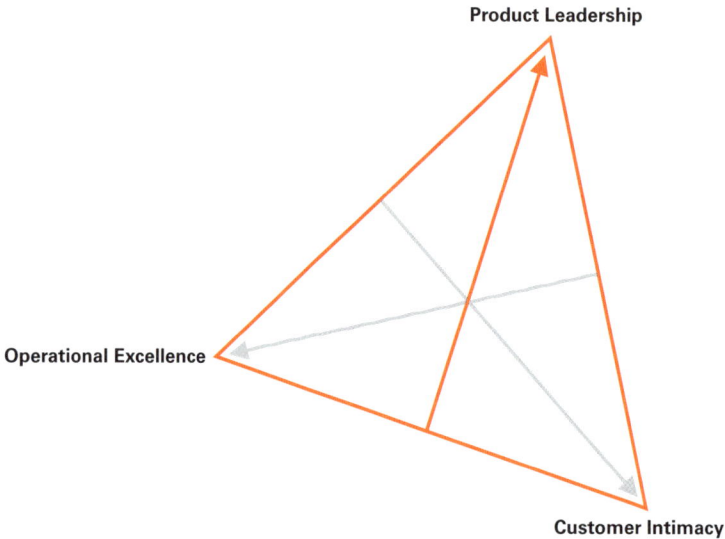

First, I like to draw the model in a slightly different way: as a triangle (Figure 37). Triangles always reflect choices to be made in a balance. Drawn like this, the model represents a more integrated view of the choice to be made: not only do we make ourselves visible and relevant to the outside world, but we do so by visibly creating some value. What that value is is related to what we can create, which is our identity. All dimensions of the model become interdependent in this version. In other words, the model shows that choosing a certain position has consequences for the other perspectives. Choosing a particular positioning does not 'free' us from the other two dimensions — quite the opposite. Figure 38 shows that in order to make our chosen positioning true, we need a certain value of the other two angles of that positioning. The figure shows a choice for product leadership; this means that we must have our homework done for our operational excellence and our customer intimacy, otherwise we will not deliver the quality required for this leadership. We need to get our processes right and have a clear understanding of what our customers want.

Figure 38. Interdepencies between leadership and threshold values of positioning.

In Treacy and Wiersema's terms, being distinctive or unique on one of the dimensions means having a minimum 'threshold' (credibility) on the other dimensions. This is why I called positioning an identity-driven 'mission' on the 'inside' of the organisation: if we want to achieve strong product leadership (in the case of this example), then everything we do should be geared towards that. Our processes should focus on the quality of the product, our customer and market research should tell us what needs we are meeting with our product, and the whole organisation should be focused on delivering the best product. The same applies to operational excellence or customer intimacy.

We can take this model a step further. Since Treacy and Wiersema developed it some thirty years ago, the market has changed quite radically. Today, we are much more used to more integrated services: in our networked and platformed market, we buy many things 'as a service', meaning that the sometimes highly specialised services around the product we are actually buying are part of the offer. The best known of these is 'SaaS', Software as a Service, where we no longer buy the software itself, but access to it, with the guarantee that we will always have the latest version of the software and the support we might need. And platforms like Maester take this SaaS approach one step further by offering 'Content as a Service' (and in the case of Maester, even a corresponding 'Community as a Service').

In these propositions, the interaction between seller and customer is much stronger (we get the opportunity to express our needs and 'tweak' the actual product), and in the 'background' of the delivery we see constellations of suppliers and specialists who together provide the actual services (e.g. the software developer, the support and service providers, the hosting providers, the compliance and security specialists, etc.). Of course, we could still use Treacy and Wiersema's model to position this, but then we would be ignoring the importance

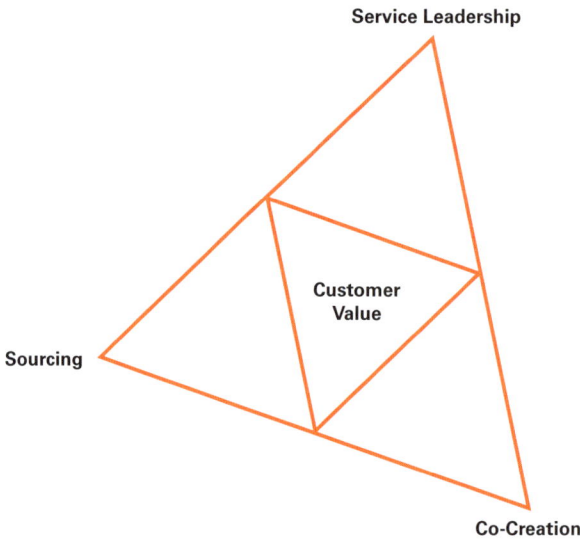

Service Leadership

Customer
Value

Sourcing

Co-Creation

Figure 39.
Positioning in
the era of hyper-
interactivity.

Note 17.
Brandt and Van
Moorst, 2010.

of the interaction between the various players on the supply and demand side. In an essay published in 2010,[17] Hans Paul Brandt and Annemiek van Moorst therefore presented a more developed version of the model, which I show in a slightly modified form in Figure 39.[18]

By rebaptising the perspectives of the model, it touches on different worlds: 'service leadership', 'sourcing' and 'co-creation' all describe a much more interactive approach to the dimensions of the original. The result, in my view, is that the model both describes what is actually happening in our current state of the marketplace, where the distinctions between supplier, partner and customer are much less defined, and also captures the interactive aspect of the identity aspect of positioning: if the mission is still to deliver on your proposition, then these interactions are also part of your organisation's identity. The boundaries between your organisation and your partners or the market are no longer as strict as you might expect; and that is precisely why you are who you are. I repeat here what I said earlier about the significance of Maester's approach: it

Note 18.
In Brandt's and
Van Moorst's
version, it
reads 'social
networking'
instead of 'co-
creation' — it
seemed to me
that, since 2010,
further adaption
of the model was
needed, since
the interaction
between
customer and
provider only has
become stronger;
and the centre
read 'customer
management',
which I changed
to 'Customer
Value' to stress
the focus on the
significance of
services for both
provider and
customer.

provides an answer to a higher demand for interactivity. In its complex area of knowledge exchange, in its close co-creation with the customer, Maester is a step forward in this networked and platformed environment. Interactivity has become part of its identity.

Modelling marketing

I promised to elaborate on the structured development of a marketing strategy using the marketing roadmap I have developed over the years (Figure 40). I explained earlier that I see branding as a process in time; a process that requires structured effort. Branding is about maintaining consistency with everything and everyone in the organisation, but it is also about giving your target audiences the opportunity to build their image of you, their personal psychological construct, the 'brain position' as it is called amongst marketers.

If this is a process, then so is the whole marketing strategy. We need to build the marketing itself, just as we build the brand. Hence the two axes of the matrix: horizontally the path to successful branding, vertically the way to develop your marketing as such.

To start with the branding process (on the horizontal axis): it all starts with your positioning. What do you want to be known for, where in the market can we find you, what needs and pains do you address, what makes you special, indispensable, unavoidable? Whether you use the positioning model we outlined earlier or something else, relevance is key. Why are you relevant and to whom?

The next step is to identify the topics and issues that are topical and important for your positioning. On what issues are you an authority, or can you develop into one? What knowledge, expertise and experience do you have that would make you visible in your market with the desired positioning? What do you know and what have you done that supports this positioning?

	Positioning	Thought leadership	Communication	Branding
Think	Central statement	Relevant issues, themes and markets	Communication strategy	Brand strategy
Create	Message house	Content	Communication building blocks	Brand building blocks
Activate	PR and PA	Publish	Means, media and channels	Campaigning
Prove	Participation level	Visible dialogue	Monitoring (share and domain)	Monitoring (recognition, NPS)

The third step is to identify the right communication for the positioning. What do you want who to understand about us and what 'style', frequency and level of communication would be appropriate? And the final step is to think about branding itself: how can we use the brand itself to position ourselves, and what impact would that have on the target audience's image of you?

The vertical axis is quite simple: first, we need to conceptualise our marketing approach, to develop the 'big ideas' at the abstract, strategic level. Second, we create the building blocks to manifest those ideas. Thirdly, we activate these building blocks in the four areas of our marketing strategy. And finally, we measure what is happening as a result of our marketing, allowing us to consider whether we need to adjust or even pivot our efforts.

The cells now become apparent. When we Think about our positioning, we formulate our central statement, like the pay-off or the boilerplate, which describes us in our essence and in our desired position. Thinking about our thought leadership will lead us to the relevant themes, issues and market knowledge

Figure 40.
The marketing matrix.

that we need to make our own and turn into our contribution to the 'discourse' in our market. And thinking about our communications and branding will lead us to devise strategies for them.

The 'Create' line is all about building blocks: basic elements that we can use to activate our marketing. The message house contains our basic message to the world in different lengths and versions: the pay-off (one line describing the added value for the domain), the boilerplate (a paragraph on the essence of the organisation and its proposition), the one-pager (a more detailed description), a detailed Q&A — they elaborate on the same message over and over again. Content (to achieve thought leadership) needs to be available in a variety of lengths and formats: from blogs to white papers, and from short web texts to lengthy presentations and discussion papers. Communication building blocks are not just text, but also the way we present ourselves, the means by which we seek to influence the knowledge, attitudes and behaviours of our target audiences. And brand building blocks are the brand itself in its visual environment, but also more intangible aspects like tone of voice, vocabulary, moments and places where we want to be present, et cetera.

Activation is where we find marketing in action. This is where we perform on a daily basis. PR (our direct contacts that influence our relationships and create goodwill for our organisation) and PA (our protocols and actions when things go wrong), our publications of the content we create (and continue to create), our communication in all its aspects: what means do we use, where and when do we use them, through whom, etc., and our campaigns: direct, actively propelled communication efforts related to our brand, e.g. through social media or outdoor media.

There is no point in marketing if you do not measure your impact. We can monitor whether our positioning is successful by looking at our participation in the market: our market share, our influence on the development of the market, the reaction of competitors and partners, and so on: to what extent are we a player in this market? The same goes for our thought leadership: are our ideas on the topics and issues being well received, taken forward, responded to? Communication and branding call for structured monitoring (for which there are many tools, ranging from media monitoring to engagement reports); but where communication calls for monitoring the share and domain of the communication itself, for our branding we need to monitor the significance for ourselves as an organisation (at the brand level, that is): to what extent are we recognised, what is our NPS score, et cetera.

Having such a very structured approach to your marketing has two related advantages: on the one hand, it makes for efficiency and effectiveness, as everything is coordinated and consistent, there is no duplication or wasted effort; at the same time, it ensures that everything you do is in line with your positioning and ambitions, with your identity as the centrepiece of everything you do to connect with your environment.

Looking back at Maester's marketing roadmap, we can see how all of its marketing actually stems from its central positioning statement 'Leren van elkaar' (Learning from each other): the themes are clear, the communication and branding strategy aims for maximum interactivity, content is co-created with the community, and above all: the platform itself is the dominant channel through which the marketing process takes place. Everyone learns from everyone else — including Maester itself. This makes for a very solid, trustworthy and unifying positioning.

Positioning is choosing.

The best way to become a market leader is define your own market.

If values are upheld, ambitions are accepted.

Strong brands do not explain themselves but grow in attributed significance.

The current level of interactivity in the market fits well with the essential character of identity.

Braking brands

When we reflect on the genesis of organisations, we see an iterative and continuous progress, in which the environment and the own origins are the boundaries of the meandering path that the organisation follows. Such a process cannot be captured in a brand. Brands must remain true to themselves. Brands must show themselves consistently at every moment and in front of every target group and therefore point backwards and not ahead. They always refer to themselves and do not allow interaction. Brands are hermetic in nature. Their development and growth lie beyond themselves: in the heads and the hearts of the target groups of the organisation. And the question is of course whether development is a necessity for a brand. It is not their role to learn. Brand growth is an increase in perception, not in significance.
What if there were no brands? Then there would be just people and ideas. If brands serve as a link between people and ideas, and we find that brands are limited in that they cannot develop themselves by their own nature, then in the identity domain we look for alternative connections. We look at the whole of the shared space in which people and ideas are located and find the points of contact. We discover where we coincide in our shared space and recognise each other there. We look at social, cultural and ethical values. We meet on the basis of character.

Identity as a sensing model.

Service design and the monitoring of relevance.

How a sector organisation in healthcare manages the interests of the members and its stakeholders.

Defining identity-based services, core stakeholders and stakeholder journeys.

6

Identity can show your relevance.

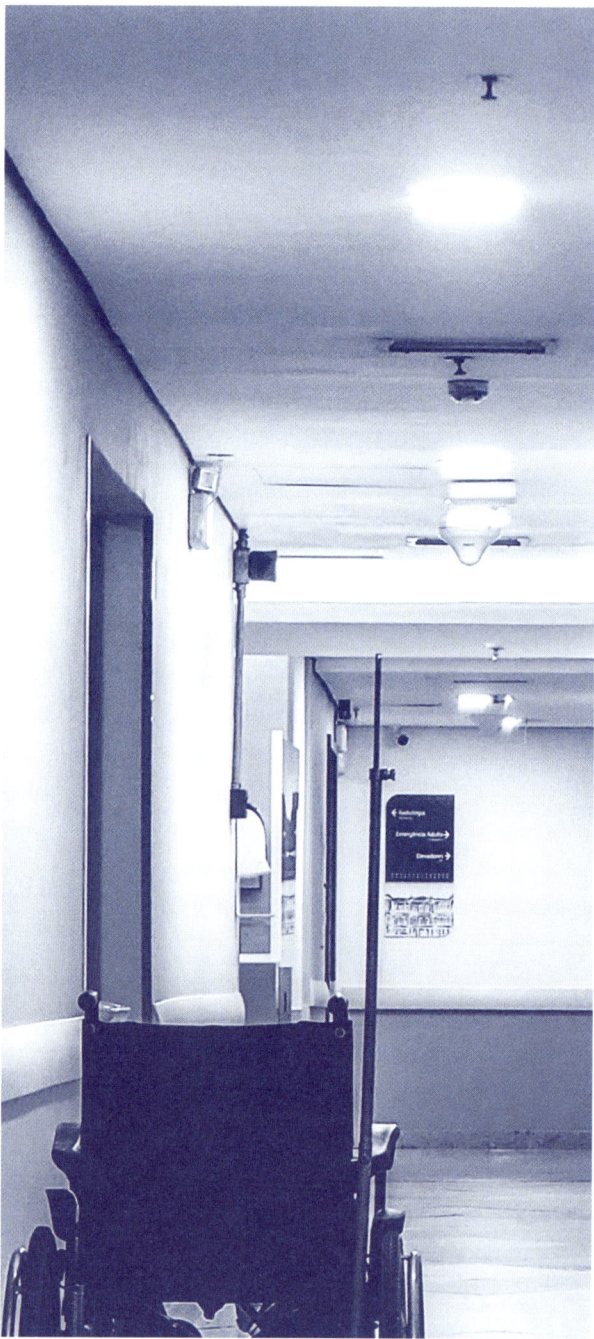

A national healthcare sector association.

How creating value created a position.

In the description of the Tergooi case in Chapter 3, I briefly explained the rather complicated structure and context of the healthcare sector in the Netherlands. It is a situation to which each care and cure provider has to find answers individually, depending on its specific role, situation and ambitions; but at the same time there are issues and themes that are relevant to all healthcare institutions. Think of the ever-changing landscape, the rapidly growing demand for care, the common political interests of all players in the sector, financial constraints, the complicated situation on the labour market, or market or quality regulations at national level.

Clearly, the pressures on the healthcare sector are enormous. We have an ageing population, which means fewer people to pay for more healthcare: as people live longer, they will need more treatment in later life, while at the same time the proportion of the population that is working is falling. We see problems with obesity, diabetes and other lifestyle diseases. We see the effects of urbanisation, pollution and climate change. We have come through a covid pandemic that has left deep scars on the healthcare landscape and demands a preventative response to the next pandemic that is sure to come. Promising technology continues to drive up costs. The labour market is very challenging, to say the least; even if we could pay for all these developments, we would not have the people to do the work. And so on.

In the Netherlands we speak of 'lines' of healthcare to describe roles and responsibilities in both care and cure. The 'first line' is the healthcare you can go to without a referral and is made up of general practitioners, dentists, physiotherapists, pharmacists, social workers and district nurses. They are the gateway to the health system and triage patients and clients who need to go 'deeper'. Second line care is provided by any provider that requires a referral: for example, specialists in hospitals or clinics, as well as specialist rehabilitation and mental health services. They deal with the more complicated problems identified by the first line professionals. The 'third line' includes academic hospitals and specialist centres, for example for extremely complex illnesses and treatments. They are highly specialised supporters of the second line. We can also identify a 'fourth line' of even more specialised medical professionals (a rare species) and a 'zero line', the healthcare that is always there, without individual demand: e.g. municipal health services that monitor growing children, provide vaccinations and preventive services, among many others. In addition, there is a system of subsidies for 'informal care', i.e. care provided by family, friends and neighbours to people whose physical or mental health prevents them from functioning independently.

Let me give you a few examples of the complexity of what may seem clear and simple in this enumeration, but which creates all sorts of inefficiencies and even health risks.
We are seeing the development of what is known as the 'one-and-a-half line' of healthcare: close collaboration between GPs and specialists in GP practices. This is one of the typical attempts to reduce costs and improve efficiency, under the umbrella of a national programme called 'The right care in the right place': the idea that we should provide healthcare in the specific place in the healthcare chain that is best equipped to do so, either in terms of quality standards, volume, expertise or facilities. We are also seeing the development of the concept of 'sensible care': providing healthcare that makes sense, eliminating unnecessary treatments or even deciding not to treat (e.g. if someone would come out of treatment worse than they went in).
After long negotiations, we have come up with an 'Integrated Healthcare Agreement' between all the professionals and institutions in the different lines, to try to get them to work together in a more sensible and efficient way. We know that we have to rethink 'perverse incentives' such as the income model

of medical specialists, who are paid per treatment, but who are rightly reluctant to change a model on which they have planned their financial budgets. Et cetera, et cetera.

If we are to change things in our healthcare system, it is a task that is, of course, carried out in the political arena, between politicians and a number of sector associations representing the various groups of professionals and institutions. The boards of these sector organisations are usually drawn from the boards of the member organisations, and the day-to-day work is carried out by a central bureau consisting of specialists in the various areas of interest to the sector, ranging from lobbying to knowledge sharing and from facilities to advice. The sector organisations are negotiating parties in the sectoral CBAs, policy makers and contact points for politicians, communicate with all relevant stakeholders at national level, and so on. It is a complex position in which the interests of the associated members have to be represented at many levels — at the same time as these interests may be slightly different.

We worked for a number of years with one of the healthcare sector associations[19] on its positioning, presentation and communication and other strategic aspects of the organisation. One of the things I will focus on here is how we worked with the association to develop the value proposition and its link to the association's positioning and stakeholder management in what we called the 'Association Value Cycle' — see Figure 41.

Let me begin by explaining what the model says about the value that sector associations bring to their members and stakeholders; later in this chapter I will elaborate on the model itself. What we have defined as the value proposition of secrtoral associations are three dominant roles that reinforce each other and the position of the association. It is the performance of these tasks that creates the value proposition for the different stakeholder groups. Let's start

Note 19.
The association in question preferred not to be recognisably included in this book.

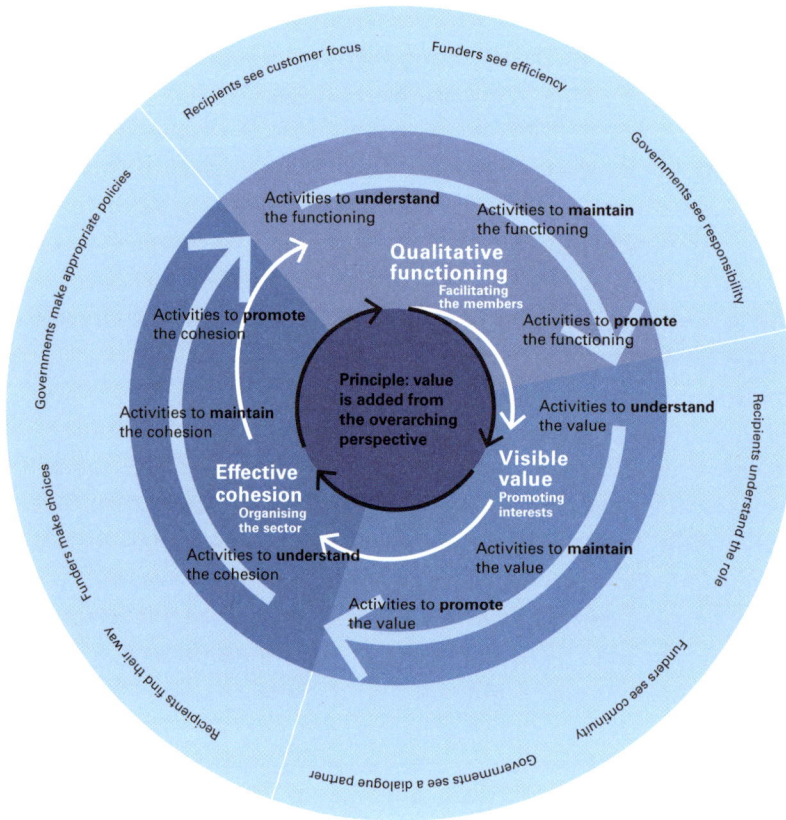

Figure 41.
Healthcare sector
association 'value
cycle'.

with the position: we argue that sector associations are formed because their members can do together what they cannot do individually. In other words, the association only does what the individual members cannot do, thus creating value for the members from an 'overarching perspective'. In other words, the position is to some extent the proposition.

We also looked at how the classic roles of any sector organisation — supporting members, organising the sector and promoting the interests of the sector and its members — fit with this proposition. We redefined these tasks in terms of their value to stakeholders (including the members themselves):

sector organisations support the qualitative functioning of the sector (by facilitating their members), demonstrate the value of their sector as such (by promoting its interests) and promote the cohesion of the sector (by organising it). The interesting thing is that these roles and values then begin to reinforce each other, creating a value proposition in the form of a flywheel: qualitative functioning increases the value of the sector, which in turn influences its cohesion and functioning. By fulfilling its missions, the association creates a common, visible and quality culture and sector proposition.

In order to understand what these roles and values mean to external stakeholders and to organise the initiatives and activities of the associations, we identify three 'stages': understanding, maintaining and promoting. For example, to understand the value of the sector to its stakeholders, the sector associations carry out continuous research and publish the results; to maintain this value, they organise typical events such as network meetings and congresses; and to promote this value, they organise specific events and participate in relevant third-party bodies. We then defined the main external stakeholders in healthcare as 'recipients', 'funders' and 'governments' and asked ourselves what they might see or think of the healthcare sector through the efforts of the associations. We found values such as 'Recipients will understand the role these providers play in the healthcare sector', 'Funders will trust their continuity' and 'Governments will see a dialogue partner'.

However, this representation of position, value proposition and tasks is more than just a representation of tasks and structures. Precisely because the work of the sector association creates links between the members of the sector and external stakeholders, and because it performs the relevant tasks, the value cycle also functions as a sensing model. It organises the links between a wide range of internal and external

THE MEMBERS' COLLECTIVE	THE INDIVIDUAL MEMBER	THE STAKEHOLDER	THE EMPLOYEE
Hans, 55, settled executive with end-responsibility for an organisation. He has an academic level of thinking, is self-assured, convinced of his own strengths and abilities, has a professional attitude. He asks us questions to which he wants clear answers. He is critical and demands a service-minded attitude: we are there for him. He wants to achieve his own goals with our support and is therefore not easily satisfied: his ambitions are outspoken and grow by the day. He is a customer and remains customer - simply because when you are a member, you stay a member.	Maarten, early 50s, MT member. Is knowledgeable about content, but still sometimes stumbles over process. Has managerial responsibilities and explicitly asks for support in his decision-making: under the confident attitude, there is nevertheless some uncertainty. His questions usually come in the form of orders, he readily demands commitment from his Association, exploits our knowledge, expects us to be up to date on current affairs, has discovered that we serve his personal interests. He is not easily satisfied, sometimes finds us lacking in speed and accuracy, but is of course a loyal member.	André is a director of 45, a typical senior: intellectual but decisive. He represents a constituency relevant to us and has responsibility for one or more dossiers. He comes to us to gain access to the sector; we are his interlocutor. André knows what he wants, is respectful but does force something on us. He is content-driven, likes to work through his issues with us in a businesslike manner and at a fast pace, and sometimes finds us not alert and up-to-date enough. Nevertheless, he remains a customer, because for him we represent a large and powerful constituency in which he needs support.	Gerard, over 40, has a substantive responsibility and gives substance to our core values. He is knowledgeable, comes from the industry and has a social drive. He asks critical questions to serve the interests of the Association (and maintain his own position within it). The heart for healthcare that characterises our Association is ultimately found in him: he has a strong conviction that what he does, matters. His work consists of researching, analysing, weighing up and deciding - all in the interests of a well-functioning healthcare sector.

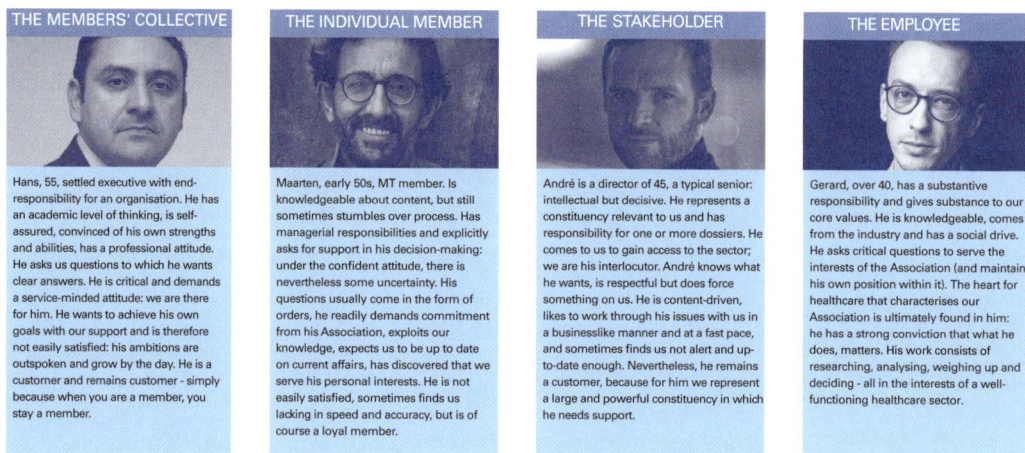

stakeholders, while monitoring the relationships and the perceived value of the association. If an initiative or activity is not relevant enough, the response will tell you so. If members are unhappy with the political lobby and don't see their interests being effectively represented, they will rebel. And if stakeholders don't see the value of the association, they won't engage with it. All the time, the actual efforts of the association provide it with signals about its value. And relevance is the key. 'What do you mean to me?' is the general question that stakeholders will ask.

Then we started to look more closely at these relationships. After all, we saw them as being of vital value to associations. The investigation took the form of defining customer profiles and customer journeys. (I'll give more insight into how I see these from an identity perspective later in this chapter) and was again done in close collaboration with the sector organisation we were working for.

We identified four core customers for sector organisations: the members as a collective, the individual members, the external stakeholders in general and the association's staff,

Figure 42.
Association core customers.

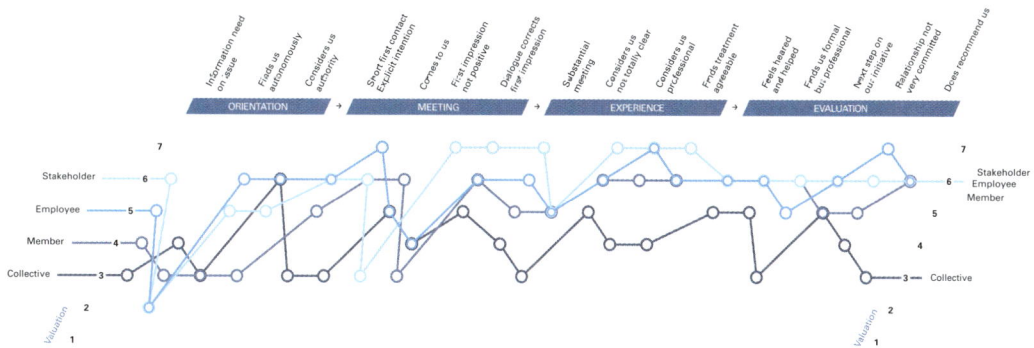

and described them as real people. We gave them names, characters, backgrounds and ambitions. We created anchor points to relate to. And then we asked ourselves what these four people experienced in their relationship with this sector organisation in their customer journey.

The association we worked with described a true and honest picture of its interactions with these four core customers. It was quite hard on itself and did not hesitate to mention the weak points in its collaboration with the 'customers'. As a result, we were able to identify the expected value and behaviour that this sector association should deliver in the eyes of its stakeholders. And the conclusion we drew was that sector organisations in general run the risk of becoming a little distant from their customer base and of acting too independently.

This conclusion drew attention to the identity of this sector association. The question arose as to the extent to which an association is the 'property' of its members and only has to respond to their demands, or whether a certain degree of independence is indispensable for the quality of its service to those members. At the same time, associations need to ask

Figure 43.
Association
customer journey
(summarised).

themselves whether the quality they are delivering is high and visible enough. The service may be very valuable but invisible. In some cases, there is a general need to professionalise the representation of the association, its activities and its communication in order to make its relevance clearer.

So we worked on the visual and communicative representation of the association, developing a very communicative visual identity that showed the association as the focal point of the sector for its stakeholders. We supported the clarity and visibility of the association's activities, e.g. through the development of an 'explanatory' style, a much more communicative design of the CBA and other regular sector publications, developed a system of corporate publications showing the association's activities and value, supported and designed campaigns et cetera. But we also worked together on the development of strategy and strategic publications and white papers, commissioning and presenting the results of research carried out by the association's office, and giving visible meaning to these results. In short, we worked with the association to build a communicative and interactive layer of activities and initiatives that made it clearer what the association actually meant to the sector as a whole, to its individual members and to its external stakeholders.

Finally, let's go back to where we started: a sector association's position is partly its proposition. Here too we see a conduct principle : 'We only do what our members cannot do for themselves and add value from an overarching perspective that only we can have'. This principle requires, on the one hand, a clear definition of the value to be delivered, which can be described in the value cycle, and, on the other hand, a good view of the competencies that the association needs to have in order to deliver that value. So we developed a vision of these to help the sector organisation maintain and develop these competencies. We made a distinction between

		We	Me
Core Question		Is everything we do aimed at helping our members to provide good care?	Do I understand at any time what our members need?
Core Commission		We set ourselves the task of helping members provide good care	In everything I do, I strive for optimal, clear and applicable conditions for members
Core Tasks	**Create frameworks**	We create the frameworks demanded by the sector and its stakeholders	I create frameworks by making visible what is happening
	Create optimal conditions	We create conditions that produce results thus forming places of evidence	I create conditions by making clear agreements and communicating them
	Promote interests	We promote interests by making members relevant	I represent interests by setting up the process
Core Values	**Enterprising**	We develop a vision and stick to it. In it, we take the initiative, use our expertise, speak out clearly, make visible what the interests and requirements are, and connect parties to each other	I develop my own vision and connect parties to it
	Expert		I am an expert in my field and portfolio
	Outspoken		I always speak out in favour of our members
	Connecting		I connect interests to achieve results
	Visible		I make goals, expectations and results visible

Figure 44.
Association core competences.

the competencies of the whole association and those of each individual employee, and organised them according to the core challenge of the sector, the mission given to the associations, and the core tasks we described earlier, but which we translated into actions to be taken by the associations and their employees. This scheme can serve as a touchstone and a monitoring tool for the development of the sector associations towards the professionalisation they may need. In other words, we have come full circle by linking the promise of the sector organisations to the mission they set themselves by making that promise. We have linked ambition to interaction; both sides of the identity coin.

Identity aspects

Associations like the one we have worked for are, I think, a clear example of the key value of relevance. You could say that a sector association acquires its value simply by existing. At the same time, this value has to be maintained and demonstrated: the association has to stay relevant — which is hard work. Moreover, being relevant to your stakeholders (both internal and external) links the external promise to the internal mission of the organisation. In other words, it links the organisation's positioning to its leadership and competencies. Then there's the hard work: relevance requires vigilance, sensitivity and a certain sharpness from the whole organisation.

The way we see this association meeting this challenge is by aligning the value proposition of the organisation with the resulting conduct principle and the competencies the organisation needs: if our value is to do the things that our individual members cannot do, we turn that value into our conduct principle ('We only do those things for which we can offer an overarching perspective') and develop the competencies to deliver on that promise: the ability to respond to the key challenge of the sector and its members and to translate that challenge into values, domains and activities. Perhaps the link between relevance and identity could be summarised as 'For your stakeholders, you are what you mean to them' or, conversely, 'Our value to our stakeholders lies in our ability to deliver on our mission'. If this flywheel works well, the mission will strengthen the organisation's position, and vice versa.

The responsibilities of a sector association are considerable, as its members depend on it for some of their success. Explaining to the outside world how a particular sector works and is organised; promoting its interests in the political and business arenas; providing essential facilities such as knowledge management or validation of new developments and initiatives that would be too heavy a burden for each member to carry out on its own; the links, relationships and cooperation between members — all these aspects (and many more) are vital to the vitality of the sector as a whole, but also to each individual member.

The challenge here is that a sector association needs to keep a certain distance from day-to-day practice in order to maintain an overarching perspective, but at the same time it needs to maintain close relationships with its members in order to stay aware of what is important to them. The association needs to gain and maintain the trust of its members, especially for those times when it might do or communicate something that is harder to understand from an individual member's perspective.

Consistency and quality in everything the association does is important. The association always needs to be recognisable, and to communicate a standard of quality that convinces members and makes the association trustworthy to them. Consistent patterns of communication and interaction, a high quality of presentation and of each message to the members, frequent consultation of the members are important, as well as the visibility of the people working in the association's office, their results and their arguments. Each professional association must meet the expectations of its members in order to fulfil its position and its proposition. In other words, a sectoral association must remain true to its identity: an overarching but close partner of the organisations in the sector.

To remain relevant, the sector association must have a deep understanding of its members' challenges and drivers. Not only to serve them well, but also to make the right choices for its own development and role. Relevance, like anything identifying, has two sides: it needs to be seen as such (by the surrounding 'alterities'), and it needs to be developed and nurtured (as an identifying aspect). In the case of a sector association, it needs to respond to the right challenges and be prepared for the next ones. Ongoing reflection on its own significance as a sector association will help to answer both questions at the same time. Once again we see the essentially interactive nature of identity.

The wide variety of internal and external stakeholder profiles that a sector association has seems to make it quite difficult to answer the question 'What do we mean to people?' — unless you answer it from an identity perspective. In the identity domain, we do not talk about position or proposition before we talk about character and personality ('Unternehmenspersönlichkeit', as Birkigt and Stadler call it). And by now you will have discovered that character and personality can be multifaceted and consistent at the same time. As a person, I am a father, a husband and a son; I am a professional advisor to some people and a friend to others. Whether I'm sad or happy, I'm still the same person. Like Richard Sennett's Rico, I try to be true to myself and make my character meaningful and unifying.

The same goes for organisations: they may be diverse because of their contexts — but if they stay true to their identity, they will be consistent. And just like people, organisations have an explicit interest in staying connected to their environment: it is one of their critical success factors. Perhaps even more so for sector associations, as this connectedness is a critical part of their value proposition.
To stay true to your identity, you need to reflect on your character and personality on the one hand, and your relevance to the various stakeholders on the other. You need to be recognisable in every context; you respond to every request, challenge or question from the consistent value you want to have. The association in our case study concluded that it shared core values with its members, but translated these into its overarching position and perspective; and this proved to be the way for the association to manage the dilemma between the necessary distance and the indispensable closeness to its members.

The Value Cycle
Every sector association (or branch organisation, union, etc.)
has the same core tasks: to facilitate its members through
exchanges and services, to promote the interests of the sector
in the relevant bodies and arenas, and to organise the sector as
such by building internal relationships and making its structure
comprehensible. As we have seen in the case description,
these three tasks can be linked and understood as the value
proposition of the association.
And we can go a few steps further: what does the association's
perception of these tasks tell us about its identity? What
dynamics can we discern in the way the association carries out
its tasks? What is the relevance of the association in its specific
context? How does it effectively address its stakeholders? And
how does the perception of these missions strengthen them and
the value of the association as a whole?

In this case, we answered these questions in a very contextual
way: we put the dynamics of the healthcare sector, which I
described in the introduction to the case, directly into the value
proposition: 'If these are the challenges of the sector, they
are also ours. And as a sector association, we have a specific
perspective from which to address these challenges. We need to
convince the relevant stakeholders of the value of the sector and
where to find it; we need to respond to the flood of initiatives,
programmes and demands placed on the sector with a high
quality of operation and a cohesion that balances collective and
individual interests.'

The way to do this was to make the association's identity very
clear and, therefore, relevant. The association drew attention to
itself and to the sector by being very explicit about its tasks and
by carrying them out meticulously. 'There should be no doubt
about the quality of what the sector has to offer, so we make our
stakeholders look at how well we are organised.' In this way, the
value of the sector became clear to the different stakeholders.

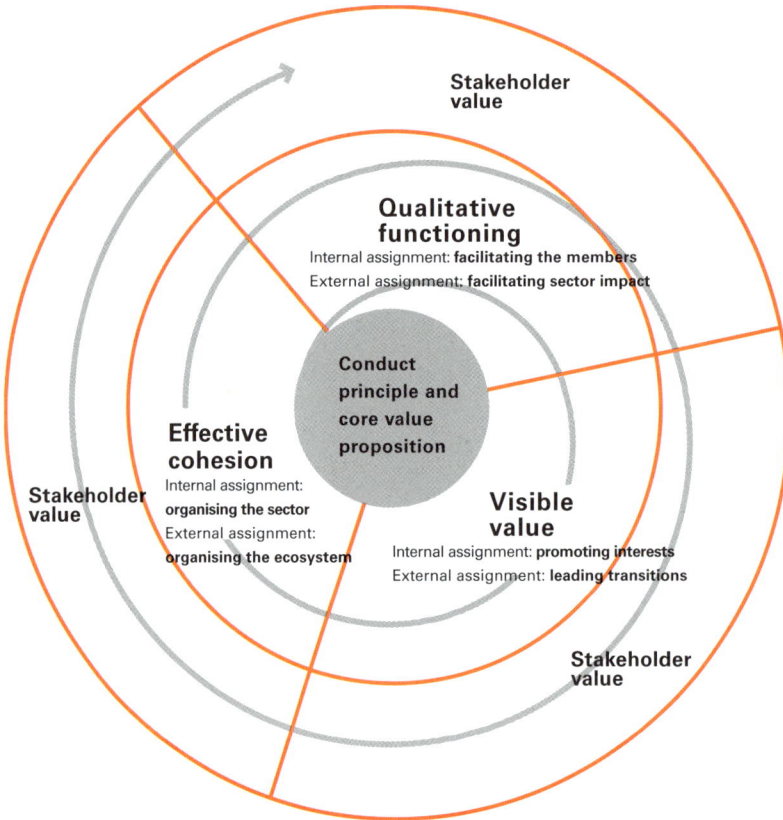

The Value Cycle model links the identity of the sector organisation with the interests and value of the sector as such: by making clear what the organisation does, it becomes clear what the sector is about and what value it delivers. The cycle distinguishes between internal and external responsibilities in all three dimensions, making it clear that a sector organisation is concerned not only with the members, interests and structure of the sector itself, but also with the surrounding context: it must take responsibility for the impact that the sector as a whole can have, for the contributions that the sector can make to the transitions that are so urgent today, and for the coherence and

Figure 45.
The Value Cycle model for (sector) associations. This is the enhanced version, containing both the internal and external assignments of a sector organisation.

	General.	Questions.
[Name.]	Is it a man or a woman? Which age? Do we know someone who resembles him/her? What is his/her professional situation? Which responsibility does he/she hold?	What kind of questions is he/she asking? To whom is he/she asking these questions? Through which channel? How does he/she get answers?
	Behaviour. What does he/she already know? How did he/she get to know us? Is he/she: Pushy | Polite | Panicky | Arrogant | Confident Empathetic | Modest | Practical |Trustful | Helpful |Open | ... | ... | ...	**Interest.** What is his/her dominant interest? What is his/her main driver? Why do we matter to him/her? Is he/she satisfied? Will he/she remain a customer? Yes | No | Do not know

Figure 46. Character based core customer description model.

dialogue of the ecosystem of which it is a part. In short, it shows how the sector organisation can (and must) show leadership on the challenges that the sector can help to solve, by leading its own members.

To achieve this, the model also combines the consistency and interactivity typical of any identity: we have a certain conduct principle that we can apply in any moment, situation or challenge. We are responsive without losing sight of ourselves. We are sensitive to our context and its dynamics precisely because we know who we are and remain true to that.

Core customer, Customer journey and Core competences
Scholars will probably never agree on whether it was Jan Carlzon, CEO of Scandinavian Airlines in 1981, Chip Bell in 1980 or Ron Zemke and Don Pepper in 1985 who originally invented customer journey mapping. But we do know that major companies such as Disney, Ikea and many others make extensive use of research into what their customers actually experience with them in order to improve their value proposition. And often the tools of customer journey mapping are used to develop a value proposition in the first place.

	Customer. **Challenge.**	Product. **Answer.**	Organisation. **Paradigm.**
Why? **Drivers.**	How does the challenge emerge?	What is it that makes us effective?	Why are we here?
What? **Objective.**	What does the challenge consist of?	What is our tangible offer?	What is our objective?
How? **Shaping.**	Where does he/she look for the answer?	How does this help the customer?	How do we intend to achieve that?

The literature on this research is extensive; I will confine myself to three tools that I use to conduct interactive research in workshop settings, whether to improve or develop the proposition. My approach is typical in that it links the character and personality of the organisation to its proposition (as you might expect): 'Who do we want to be to whom?' Hence the interactive approach: to answer this question you need perspectives from inside and outside the organisation.

The first step is to find out who your core customer is.[20] I use specific variants of a small questionnaire for this research; the one in the figure was used in the case described. The questionnaire looks at general characterisations that try to shape a real person, and then focuses on the aspects of that person that are relevant to an organisation: what are this person's interests and agenda (hidden or not)? What kind of interaction do we have with him or her? And what behaviour is typical of this person?
Taken together, the questionnaire creates a relevant picture of the customer. Sometimes there are different core customers, as in the case described. The many-headed nature of a sector organisation, which typically operates at the intersection of different domains, cannot be described by a single customer, but needs to be able to address several (and yes, I know this approach rocks the boat for some marketers).

Figure 47. Customer/ organisation interaction matrix.

Note 20. I speak about 'customer' here since this concept is the basis of all mapping; but the significance of this word to me is quite fluid; anyone with an interest in your organisation is, to some extent, a customer. For this sector association, we used the model to do the research on stakeholders of various types, which, to me, seem the customers of a sector association.

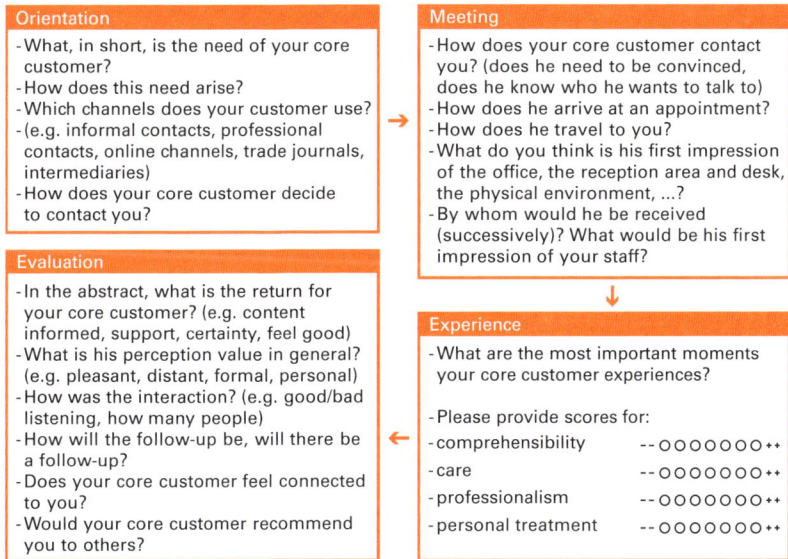

Orientation
- What, in short, is the need of your core customer?
- How does this need arise?
- Which channels does your customer use?
- (e.g. informal contacts, professional contacts, online channels, trade journals, intermediaries)
- How does your core customer decide to contact you?

Meeting
- How does your core customer contact you? (does he need to be convinced, does he know who he wants to talk to)
- How does he arrive at an appointment?
- How does he travel to you?
- What do you think is his first impression of the office, the reception area and desk, the physical environment, ...?
- By whom would he be received (successively)? What would be his first impression of your staff?

Evaluation
- In the abstract, what is the return for your core customer? (e.g. content informed, support, certainty, feel good)
- What is his perception value in general? (e.g. pleasant, distant, formal, personal)
- How was the interaction? (e.g. good/bad listening, how many people)
- How will the follow-up be, will there be a follow-up?
- Does your core customer feel connected to you?
- Would your core customer recommend you to others?

Experience
- What are the most important moments your core customer experiences?

- Please provide scores for:
- comprehensibility   -- O O O O O O O ++
- care   -- O O O O O O O ++
- professionalism   -- O O O O O O O ++
- personal treatment   -- O O O O O O O ++

A second tool I use is to describe the relationship between the customer's challenge and the organisation's character and paradigm (Figure 47). If we look at the why, how and what (thanks, Mr Sinek) of both the customer and the organisation, how does their meeting and working together address the customer's challenge? What is the value of the organisation to the customer if we look at its identity? Looking at the interactivity between the customer and the organisation in this way gives you a basic insight into how relevant you are to the customer. There are several models for describing this interactivity, such as 'value proposition design', but the simple approach I present here focuses on the identity of the organisation, and therefore describes the enduring value of the organisation as such: not of its products or services, but of its existence. It provides part of the input for the next step: mapping the customer journey.

Again, I like to use a questionnaire for this description; Figure 48 shows the version we used for the customer journey in the case description. We divided our working group into four parts, each focusing on a specific stakeholder: the members of the

Figure 48.
Customer journey mapping questionnaire.

association as a collective, the individual member, the external
stakeholder and the office staff. We focused on the relevance
of the association to these stakeholders: looking at what they
experience with us, how do they value that experience? Are we
effective, focused, attentive enough, do we really interact with
them and respond to their challenges, and so on.
The outcome of this exercise (see case study) was not
satisfactory to the association itself. 'We can do better than this',
was the conclusion. Especially since the collective of members
was seen as the most important stakeholder, but turned out to
have the lowest quality of experience.
This is why we turned to describing the competencies the
association needed to have in order to do better. By looking at
the stakeholders' experiences, we could see where the gaps
were. Describing the competences needed by the organisation
as a whole, as well as those needed by individual employees,
gave the association an improvement programme to work on.

Sensing by communicating
There are, of course, many models for describing stakeholder
environments and their dynamics. We know the 'salience' model,
which describes and compares stakeholders in terms of their
influence, urgency and legitimacy; the 'influence-impact grid',
which starts from the influence that stakeholders can have
on your organisation; the 'stakeholder analysis matrix', which
meticulously describes which stakeholders have which positions
and influence on relevant issues; the 'stakeholder participation
model', which has an almost 'bargaining' character (what do
stakeholders bring and get?); and so on. Some aspects of these
models have been incorporated into the models I have described
above.
But following my mantra that identity is interactive, I also tend
to suggest using the actual interaction of the organisation
with its environment as a field laboratory for its stakeholder
management. If we want to know what our stakeholders think
of us, why don't we look at how they react to what we do in

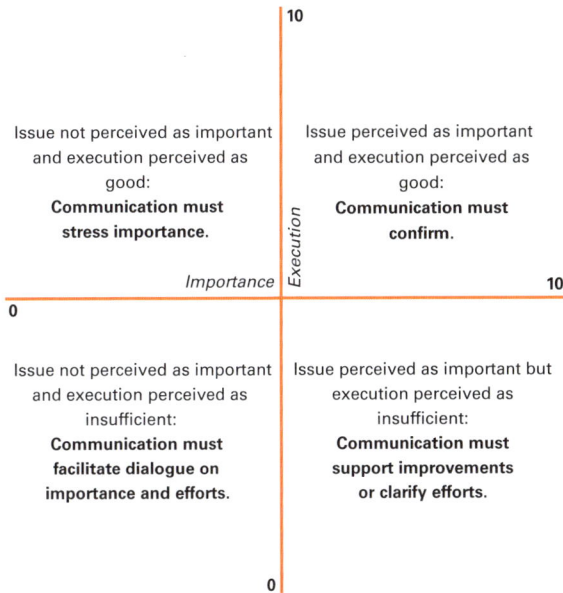

Figure 49 diagram content:

10

Issue not perceived as important
and execution perceived as
good:
**Communication must
stress importance.**

Issue perceived as important
and execution perceived as
good:
**Communication must
confirm.**

Execution

Importance

10

0

Issue not perceived as important
and execution perceived as
insufficient:
**Communication must
facilitate dialogue on
importance and efforts.**

Issue perceived as important but
execution perceived as
insufficient:
**Communication must
support improvements
or clarify efforts.**

0

Figure 49.
Image scan
valuation axes.

Note 21.
See Chapter 1
for this definition
by Birkigt and
Stadler.

real life? This approach is valuable in cases where we need to question the role and value of the organisation as such. And in the case of this sector association, as we have seen, that role and value are closely linked to its position and identity. Any response to the organisation's communication efforts is therefore an assessment of its perceived value as an organisation. Here we find a valuable sensing tool that is part and parcel of the organisation's character: 'We learn by simply doing what we do'.

To measure aspects such as these, we at Total Identity had previously developed an online tool we called the 'Image Scan', where 'image' is understood here in the sense of external perception of corporate identity.[21] The tool measures perceptions of the importance of effort on the one hand, and execution on the other, and takes into account the different stakeholder groups of an organisation and the distinctions between intuitive and reasoned responses. We used paired questions that asked respondents to indicate their view of the importance of certain competencies, initiatives and activities for the organisation in

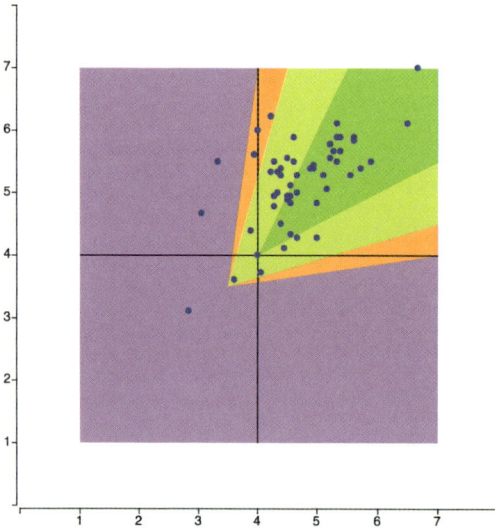

question, and their assessment of how well the organisation acted on these aspects. The results were plotted on two axes to make clear what kind of communicative attention was needed to correct or reinforce the organisation's image.
The result would typically look something like the chart in Figure 50 (this example is the image scan I did for the Dutch Senate, which gave a fairly positive result on image).

Monitoring your image and the effectiveness of your communications along these lines of importance and execution is important because you need to have a clear view of your image and positioning at all times. The results of this monitoring will tell you whether you are still doing the right things in the right way — in the eyes of your stakeholders. In other words, it will tell you if you are still relevant.

The sector association in the case description already had its own, more permanent monitoring procedures in place, so we

Figure 50.
Example of image scan results (consolidated results, based on many more underlying data and representations of the parts of which the research consisted).

did not need to carry out this particular scan, but the way in which the results were measured was quite similar. One of the activities of the association is to share information and advice on issues of concern to its members. Issues such as privacy and security in healthcare, or the growing competition between public and private healthcare providers. We advised on and co-authored white papers, developed sector-wide campaigns and co-produced all kinds of publications.

As more of these publications became digital (we are talking about the 2010s), it became increasingly possible to measure response and engagement. And the data that came from that response and engagement could be used to monitor the relevance of the association.

Assuming that the issues as such are considered important by stakeholders, low response or engagement means that it is not the issue, but the association's opinion on it, that is not very important to stakeholders. We cannot, of course, plan issue management efforts — issues tend to be unplanned — but we can see patterns in response and engagement. In this case, these taught us that a strong and outspoken opinion was generally perceived as more relevant than staying silent on the issue. Which, in turn, told us that stakeholders were demanding that the association play its role as an authority in the sector, under penalty of no longer being relevant. And it led us to present the organisation and its issue-oriented communication as a strong, outspoken and very knowledgeable partner of the healthcare system in the Netherlands.

Design principles for relevance

Connective power is born in relevancy.

To our stakeholders, we are the value we deliver.

We need to understand the experience we offer to others.

We learn by just doing what we do.

Any position holds a proposition.

Designing relevance

Letting go of your convictions is a hard thing to do, since they
are connected to who you yourself are. Convictions are the
result of a certain indispensable stubbornness of perspective,
which makes you stay true to yourself.
Allowing for flexibility and other people's insights — one of the
definitions of creativity — will also allow room for development
of who you are. Will ignite the vital interaction that shows your
identity. And show your relevance and significance, not only to
your stakeholders but also to yourself.
Service oriented development will make you connective,
evolving and authentic. After all, the value you can deliver only
shows when you deliver it.

Identity as a reference point.

The relationship between consistency, direction and goal setting.

The city of 's-Hertogenbosch engages with its inhabitants.

Social design frameworks and the programme management canvas.

7

Project, programme and process management.

Identity can be a brief.

WAT IS JE
DROOM VOOR
'S-HERTOGEN-
BOSCH?

EN HOE
MAKEN WE
DIE WAAR?

www.shertogenboschcentraal.nl

'S-HERTOGENBOSCH
CENTRAAL

City of 's-Hertogenbosch.
How a city consulted its citizens on its future.

The province of Noord-Brabant, in the south of the Netherlands, has its own special character. As Noord-Brabant and Limburg are the only predominantly Catholic provinces, this region has developed a different culture from the Netherlands 'above the big rivers', as we call it; a little more traditional, more focused on enjoying everyday life, boasting a rich community life, of which carnival is the most visible and festive expression. At the same time, Brabant is a thriving economic region, ranging from a high-tech cluster around Eindhoven with world-famous names such as Philips and ASML, to highly industrialised agriculture throughout the province (which, incidentally, is facing dramatic challenges as I write this, as this industry needs to be transformed into a more sustainable model).

The capital of Noord-Brabant is 's-Hertogenbosch, or 'Den Bosch' in everyday language. It is an 800-year-old yet lively city of just over 150,000 inhabitants, with a very attractive, well-preserved historic centre, a wide variety of residential areas and a strong position in the IT industry. In the Atlas of Municipalities, 's-Hertogenbosch was ranked number 5 as a good place to live. One of the city's ambitions is to become a leading data city; dedicated initiatives such as the Jheronimus Academy of Data Science and the Den Bosch DataWeek support this ambition. 's-Hertogenbosch is remarkably successful in combining its historical origins with its ambitions: local historical figures such as Jheronimus Bosch and the Dukes of Brabant play a role in everyday narratives and drive the artistic, cultural and entrepreneurial spirit of the city.

But sustainable success requires maintenance. In 2019, the municipality of 's-Hertogenbosch issued a European tender, asking for support in developing an 'agenda' for the city: 'With an "agenda of and for 's-Hertogenbosch" we want to hold up a mirror to ourselves, get inspiration and organise movement through participation with the city', as the tender stated. The agenda was not to be a development plan, an overarching vision or a unilateral initiative by the municipality, but a participatory process, a source of inspiration and energy from which residents, entrepreneurs and the public administration could draw in the coming years. In short, the city asked for a social design: a way of describing and activating the city's society, based on the expertise, wishes and concerns of the people who live and work in 's-Hertogenbosch. TwynstraGudde, the consultancy where I was working at the time, applied and won the tender, and I had the honour of being the project leader for the definition of the 'Bossche Agenda', as we called it.

The process was conceived in two stages: in a first round, we had to gather insights, challenges, wishes and visions from everyone with an interest in 's-Hertogenbosch: residents, entrepreneurs, local, regional and national governments, and visitors; but also sports clubs, cultural associations, social workers, employers' and entrepreneurs' associations, tourist boards, and so on. From there, we were to create an 'external mirror' of the city, as the brief put it, and facilitate a dialogue on this mirror with the same target groups.

We decided to build on two foundations: the very outspoken historical-cultural character of the city and its people, and thorough data research. We wanted to corroborate the results of a creative approach to gathering thoughts, opinions and ambitions with data from desk research, to find evidence as well as biases and misunderstandings. The data could reinforce the results of the dialogue we had with the people of 's-Hertogenbosch. Let me elaborate on this approach.

As I said, Brabant, and perhaps 's-Hertogenbosch in particular, has a very outspoken culture. Based on history and tradition, people tend to take all kinds of initiatives in groups. Cultural associations, sports teams, but also groups of entrepreneurs like to work together for common goals. And the great annual celebration of this culture is the carnival. This is the time when

all values are temporarily turned upside down, the people rule instead of the regular governors, issues and situations are sarcastically criticised and governors are taken to task. Towns and villages are rebaptised ('s-Hertogenbosch is called 'Oeteldonk' during carnival) and are temporarily ruled by Princes of Carnival, who start their three-day reign with a very sarcastic public speech about the situation of the town and its governors, after being handed the keys to the town by the regular mayor. Everyone dresses up to not look like themselves, and the towns and villages of Brabant (and Limburg) erupt in a three-day collective celebration of life, with lots of music and beer, festive processions and extravagances (followed by penance on Ash Wednesday).

This is where we started: if the people of 's-Hertogenbosch are used to having their say, and we are looking for an agenda for the city, why not ask them directly? After all, this agenda must be based on the concerns, worries, fears, insights, dreams and ambitions of the people who live and work in 's-Hertogenbosch. In other words, the very things they are accustomed to expressing their opinions about — and not just for three days a year.

Figure 51.
An example of the candid character of the 's-Hertogenbosch Carnival: mayor Jack Mikkers and his carnivalised version during the Carnival Procession.

The future agenda of a city consists of relevant themes and issues. And I would like to define 'relevant' in two steps or aspects. First question is what is going on and how does it affect us in a general sense. But secondly, I believe that

Research
Exploring on five themes (living, working, transport, care and leisure) through interviews and source research.

Data-driven interpretation
Explaining and weighing trends and issues retrieved from interviews and sources: what do the data teach us about feelings and facts?

↓

Result
's-Hertogenbosch's treasure map: the first 'external mirror'.

Result
Data and perception presented in their significance.

Deepening phase
Testing and weighing the 'external mirror' by discussing it with the city.

↓

Result
Shared and reconsidered 'external mirror': The story of 's-Hertogenbosch.

↓

Celebration
Giving the story back to the city by the competent authority: mandate for a shared future.

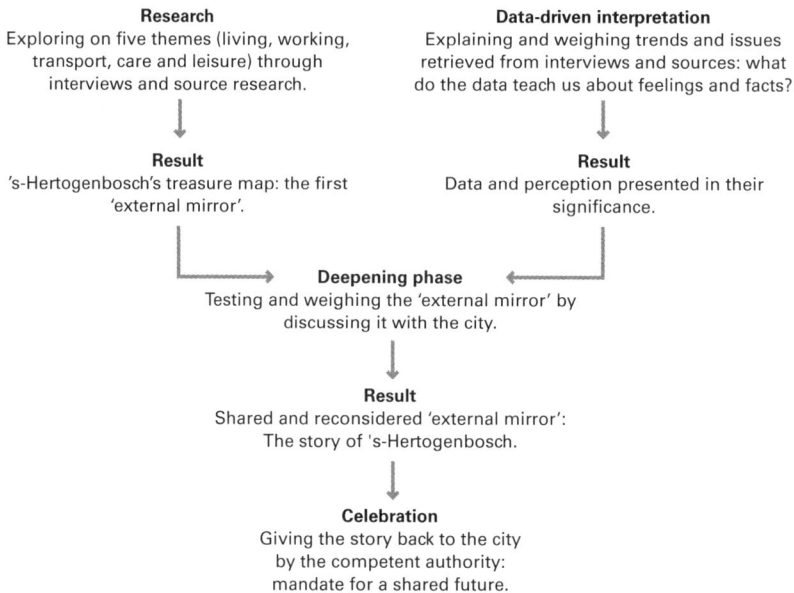

what is relevant in terms of issues and themes in this case is determined by the city's identity: what are our ambitions, how did we get them and how do we share them. In other words, we define what we want together, in an interactive process in which citizens and entrepreneurs are the experts of their own situation and the administration collects, tests, understands and activates. This is the approach that won us the contract.

We then proposed the process shown in Figure 52. In the first phase we took two paths: one path was to find and explore relevant issues along five dominant themes: living, working, moving, caring and spending leisure time in the city of 's-Hertogenbosch, using a design thinking approach to get to the core of these issues and themes; the other path was to do extensive data research to be able to understand these themes and issues in their significance and scope for the city. People tend to frame reality in terms of their personal interests, which tells us two things: that these issues have real meaning for real

Figure 52.
Schematic representation of the process we followed in the 's-Hertogenbosch citizen's consult.

people, and that we need to test them. Design thinking can help find that real meaning; data research will give it context. (I'll come back to design thinking itself and its relevance to identity later).

The combined results of these two paths could be used as input for the requested 'external mirror': an expert view from us consultants on what we think is important and crucial for the city. The second phase would then be to deepen these results by organising them into relevant themes and discussing them again with the town's residents. We proposed to celebrate the final results by presenting them as a gift from the city's residents to their governors and as a shared agenda for future decisions.

What we did in practice to get to our dialogues was to camp out in the city — literally. We 'branded' a camper van, travelled around the city for about two weeks and set it up in a number of significant places: in the city centre, at specific moments in residential areas, on sports fields, at the hospital, at weekly markets and in churches. All the time, people were invited to talk about what they thought was important to them, whether they lived or worked in 's-Hertogenbosch or visited the city. We used inviting questions, always in two parts, asking not only for importance, but also for arguments, blockades and possibilities. Questions like 'Do you like living in 's-Hertogenbosch? Why?' or 'What is your dream for 's-Hertogenbosch? And how can we make that dream come true?' or 'What makes you proud of 's-Hertogenbosch? And how can we make sure it stays that way?'

We used questionnaires, coffee with typical Brabant pastries like the famous 'Bossche Bol', umbrellas for the rain, drawing paper for the children, clever timing and a very welcoming and open attitude to get people talking and to get to the heart of the issues mentioned. People told us stories, shared their concerns and wishes, wanted to address the mayor personally, made drawings, poems and short 'tile wisdoms' (aphorisms like those

Figure 53.
The 'City
Conversations'-
travel, the results
as we got them
and the first
ordering of those
results.

How we make a living. 'Bye! We have to go to school now, we're learning for painter. Earning money, that's important!'

How we can live here pleasantly. 'Sometimes I worry for my little son.'

How we can take care of each other. 'My parents have always taken care of me, I will soon take care of them.'

How we treat each other over here. 'The city must remain open to all.'

What about downtown. 'Living in the city centre is super. Always something to do.'

How we ensure good facilities. 'It would be really good if the neighbourhoods got their own welcoming facilities.'

How we think about conservation and renewal. 'A beautiful skyline: tall buildings behind the historic centre; that would make 's-Hertogenbosch really cool in the future.'

How we can pursue sustainability. 'I wish everyone a well-insulated home, in summer and in winter.'

found on the famous Delft Blue tiles). We ended up with a huge number of insights, wishes and concerns in various formats, which we then sorted and summarised to get to the heart of things.

The power of working from a design perspective, as we did, is that you open up any conversation; you do not focus on a rationalised, direct answer to your questions (which limits you to just that answer), but use open questions as conversation starters. Social designers believe that people are the experts of their own situation. They will share their personal insights, visions, challenges and dreams. They will tell you stories, give you examples, be examples themselves, give you insight into their successes and their problems. You will find real problems for real people, not categories or abstract versions of these problems and people.

Box 1.
The themes
from the City
Conversations.

Through our City Conversations we found eight dominant 'themes of wishes and worries', as we called them (see Box 1). The themes themselves may not seem very surprising — the way they were enriched by people's views on them, their stories and examples, was. These were issues of real, everyday importance to the people who live and work in 's-Hertogenbosch. If someone says to you: 'Sometimes I worry about my little son', this is of course an absolute conversation starter that leads you into the realm of personal concerns, desires and values: what exactly is there to worry about? Why is this important to this mother? What are her expectations of life? What does she want for her son? Et cetera. And if someone says, 'It would be really good if the neighbourhoods had their own welcoming facilities', it means that in their perception these facilities are not there and could bring value. What kind of value? Why do we need facilities at the neighbourhood level? What does the neighbourhood mean to them? What is this daily environment, and why is that important enough to bring up in this conversation? And so on. Diving deep into the empathic realm gives you insights that we will never have at a political or cognitive level. We begin to see and understand real people and their real challenges.

At the same time, some of my colleagues had the difficult and rather ungrateful task of doing the data research to support, understand and interpret the results of the City Conversations. They compiled an extensive data document based on the five 'megatrends' defined by PwC and translated these into 10 trends relevant to 's-Hertogenbosch. We found trends such as 'demographic change', 'housing shortage', 'increasing pressure from tourism' and 'social change and polarisation'.

For each trend, they looked for relevant data for 's-Hertogenbosch: How does this trend affect the city and its inhabitants? Where can we find examples of the consequences and how can we make projections from what we have found that are relevant for the future of 's-Hertogenbosch? How does 's-Hertogenbosch compare with other cities in Brabant? And how do these trends relate to the results of the City Conversations, do we see them coming back there?

By combining the results of the City Conversations with those of the data document, we produced the 'external mirror' that the city had asked for. We identified strengths and weaknesses, opportunities and challenges. We compared global, regional and local trends with the results of the City Conversations. We found that the themes from these conversations were indeed the most relevant ones, also seen from the researched context, but enriched by the data with possibilities and impossibilities, initiatives and policies, in short, by their conditional context. We understood why these issues were problematic and important to people.
So we summarised everything in eight 'design challenges', which followed the lines of the themes we found (see Box 2 on next page).

The format of a challenge is important here: these are issues that we need to solve together as a city, not in a top-down way, but with the involvement and participation of everyone. We need the real expertise and knowledge base that we find in the people who are involved in these issues simply by living and working in this city, and who see working on these issues as a common interest. In other words, these are not tasks for the city government, but for the city as a whole. And by framing each question in the typical 'design challenge' format, which always starts with 'How can we...', we ensure that the issue is open to everyone and every approach, because this formulation does not exclude any person, view, thought or strategy.

When we presented the results of our work to the city council, we encountered some typical difficulties in applying a design approach to the public domain. As my TwynstraGudde colleague André Schaminée describes in detail in his then recently published book,[22] the distance between people working in the public domain and designers or creative strategists can be quite large. If you are used to cognitive approaches, where you rationalise your way to a solution,

Note 22.
Schaminée, 2018.

How can we make a living so that everyone (now and in the future) can participate in
our prosperity?
How and where do we work, where do we make money as a city, how do we ensure
that everyone can participate, how do we ensure that our earning model does not put
pressure on the quality of our environment, ...

How can we ensure that everyone enjoys living here — now and in the future?
How do we ensure sufficient and good housing — also for first-time buyers, how
do we guarantee the quality of life in neighbourhoods, what needs to be done to
our infrastructure, how do we ensure sufficient greenery and good recreational
opportunities in a densely populated area, ...

How can we continue to take good care of each other when more and more care is
required from fewer and fewer people who can provide that care?
What do we do ourselves and what do we expect from others, how do we keep
care manageable and affordable, are there typical patterns and traditions from
's-Hertogenbosch that we could make use of, how do we divide burdens neatly, ...

How can we ensure that everyone feels at home here?
What manners do we want to have, what exactly is our culture, how do we ensure that
our networks connect instead of exclude, ...

How do we ensure that our inner city is there for everyone?
What facilities should our inner city offer, how do we ensure good accessibility, what
should be close by for the inhabitants of the surrounding villages and what can be
further away, how do we find the right balance between the inner city as a place of
gathering and as a residential area, ...

How do we ensure that we offer all that is necessary to all residents of
's-Hertogenbosch?
What quality and spread should our retail offer have, how do we guarantee good
schools in sufficient locations, how do we see the future of our libraries, cultural
institutions, sports facilities and so on, ...

How do we renew 's-Hertogenbosch with respect for the past?
What do we want to preserve and what is needed to do so, what must be made future-
proof and which interventions are necessary, how do we find the balance between
historical structures and contemporary or future needs, what can we learn from how
our forefathers dealt with the city, ...

How can we ensure that a sustainable existence becomes a reality for everyone?
Who do we consider responsible for what, what do we consider urgent and what can
wait, how do we bear the costs and how do we help each other to make sustainability
affordable for everyone, what opportunities for prosperity do we see in sustainability,
...

Box 2.
The eight 'Design
Challenges' from
the 'External
Mirror'.

or political approaches, where you negotiate your way to a solution, a design approach is hard to understand because it does not give you a solution. It will give you an insight into the deeper drivers behind what people think and do, make you understand the question at a much deeper level, help you keep an open mind — but it will not come to an end point.

So there was some rebellion in the Town Hall meetings: what exactly were we offering in these findings that the Council, as the legal representative of the people, did not already know? The answer we gave, that we were replacing categories, abstractions and political positions, did not convince them at first, because they could not see what we were offering instead. Only when we explained how these challenges were seen by real people, what they meant to them in their daily lives, how in many cases they had ideas about them or were even working on solutions themselves, not waiting for the government to do so, and so on, did the Council begin to understand the value of what we were doing.

The next steps in the process were taken by the community itself and facilitated by us. What was needed from here was to discuss the design challenges in expert groups. We needed input, insights, knowledge of developments and plans, etc., from expert parties such as the Chamber of Commerce, builders, water board governors, urban planners, ecologists, you name it; but also from the other experts that we had brought in: residents of the different areas of the city, tourists, people who work in the hospital or in the sports clubs, and so on. We needed to continue the open conversations, but this time with a focus on the specific challenges we had identified.

To facilitate these conversations, we developed an infographic version of the challenges, combining a description of the challenges themselves, relevant data and some exemplary experiences and insights we had gathered in the City

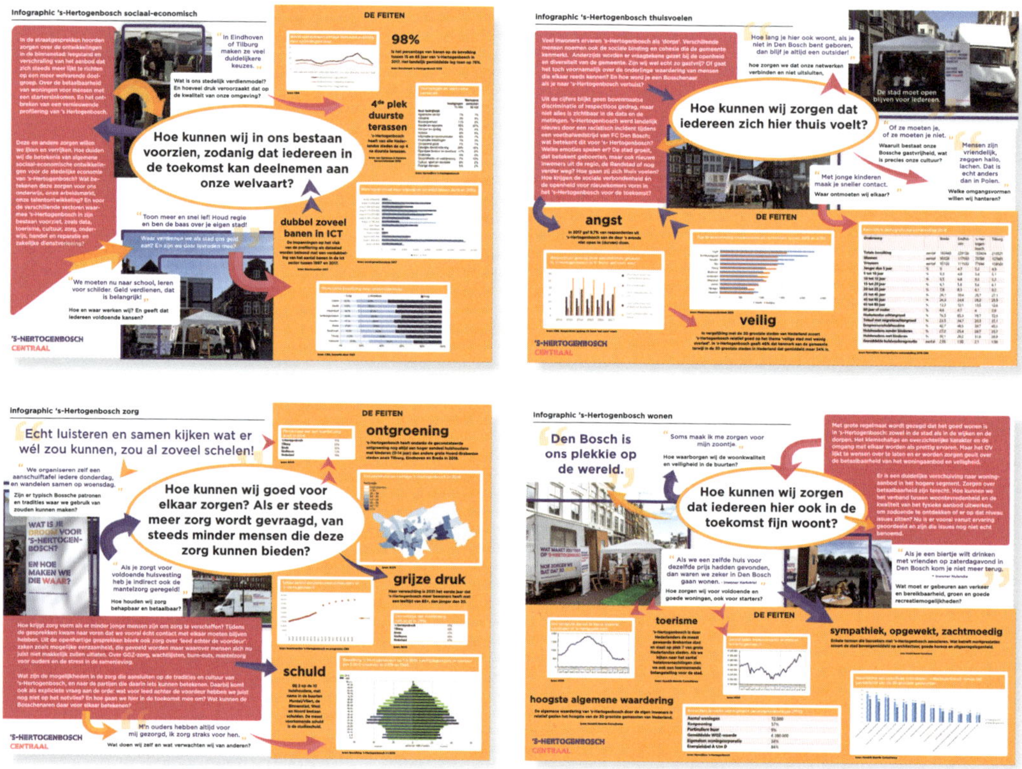

Conversations. With this step we turned the 'external mirror' into an agenda as requested: the outcome of this second phase of conversations was to answer questions like 'what can we do' and 'how can we do that'.

And that was the end of our assignment. The city took up the challenges we defined during the project and included them, among other things, in the 'Bestuursakkoord' ('Governing Agreement') of the city council, which started in 2022 and defined participation and co-creation with the residents and entrepreneurs of 's-Hertogenbosch as essential. Now the real hard work could begin.

Figure 54.
Some of the infographics we developed as conversation pieces in the second phase of the project.

Identity aspects

Eight hundred years of history is not nothing, especially when that history still plays a part in the present. Centuries of coexistence, war and peace, culture, economic development and technological advancement have surely shaped you as a city — and as a community. It would be easy to think of origins as the 'original version' of who you are now; but in reality you are what you have become in the meantime. I mentioned earlier that identity gives consistency to development: no matter how you respond to a changing context, you will inevitably remain you. Identity is a point of reference, not only in the dynamics around you, but also in time (say, eight hundred years) and space (say, in Brabant).

I was struck by the consistency of the development that 's-Hertogenbosch has gone through, simply by being proud of its origins. The history of this town shows the renewal of the same values: a strong community spirit, a tendency to grab life by the throat and enjoy it, the ability to combine a somewhat ironic view of life with a strong commitment to the community. I doubt that people who visited the city in the 1500s would have felt anything other than what we do today, but the city as such has of course changed completely. This is precisely the link between constancy and evolution that identity provides; whatever happens, your identity will always refer back to itself and its values..

A city is perhaps one of the best examples of how development, as we humans see it, is never finished. There is no moment when you can declare the city finished. There will always be new challenges, visions, opportunities and needs. This is why we chose a design approach for the development of the Agenda for 's-Hertogenbosch: because this approach also has an open end. In a design thinking process you do not work towards a solution, you work towards a real and thorough understanding of the question. Thinking about the next steps for a city requires both humility and courage: you are taking a step in a historical development that is of course bigger than you; at the same

time, every city has developed by imagining possible futures.
It took the people of 's-Hertogenbosch 160 years to build their
cathedral, and all the time they were imagining the end result
in order to persevere. But I am sure of one thing: the end result
was not exactly what they had in mind when they started. This is
what design thinking deliberately does: it creates a course rather
than a path to an end goal. We take a direction and see where it
takes us. We keep an open mind to respond to what happens in
between, to what we find along the way, to changing opinions, to
interesting ideas and visions, to unforeseen possibilities.

This is what we needed in the creation of this 'Agenda': not
being sure of the end result was essential in order not to follow
the already known lines of political or more cognitive ideas and
visions. We needed an open mind, a genuine and empathic
interest in what people knew, felt, expressed and told us. Only in
this way could we reconnect continuity and development; only
in this way could the development of the city be true to itself.
We created a dimension of development; not a project towards a
clearly stated goal. Because that is how cities evolve.

Before we started, we were of course aware of the distance
between our approach and what politicians and civil servants
knew. It was one of our own challenges to keep everyone
connected and convinced of what we were doing. If you take the
liberty to investigate freely, to allow for deliberate detours and
to include things that at first sight seem irrelevant, you run the
risk that people will not follow your efforts; after all, where will it
lead? I explained where it actually led in the case description, but
I would like to add here that such a creative approach requires a
lot of commitment from both the people doing the project and
those responsible for commissioning it.

We were very fortunate to work with experienced designers
and researchers on the one hand, and more importantly, a
committed client on the other. Whenever the going got tough,

as it did during the presentation to the council, our clients stood firm in their belief in the approach. The officials we worked with in the project group, right up to the Mayor himself, defended the approach and asked for leeway and understanding whenever needed. I learnt that this kind of relationship is essential for a creative approach in a political context. And that, in turn, the identity of that context is important: the open culture of 's-Hertogenbosch is of course also reflected in the political relationships, and that helped to make the project a success.

A final, brief, identity-related comment I would like to make here is the value that social design (I will come back to this later) can have in finding authenticity, character or values, in short: identity. Designers don't stop at the easy answers; they naturally want to go deep. They want to understand where those answers come from, find the deeper drivers, develop empathy along with the actual knowledge to be able to answer broader questions than the ones they were originally asked. You will almost immediately touch on people's values, and as we know, values are the basis of identity. Social design research is therefore very useful in uncovering a community's identity; after all, communities exist because the people in them share values and make them explicit. And in the case of 's-Hertogenbosch, very explicit.

Social engineering

Reading between the lines of the last comment above, you can sense something of my view of social design, namely that it is not the exclusive domain of a social designer. For me, it is a shared working space between designers (who facilitate the process) and the people who are affected by certain situations, developments or policies. I do not believe that social designers figure out what needs to be done in a particular case or situation, but I do believe that they are the experts in making explicit and tangible the options, ambitions, worries and wishes of the various stakeholders. And that these stakeholders all have their own indispensable role to play in the development of society.

In this sense, social design could be defined as the conscious
shaping of society, social structures and social dynamics from
the point of view of mutual benefit. Of course, this is only
possible to a limited extent; as I said before, social design does
not aim at solutions, but tries to understand the question in
depth in order to choose the right direction of development. The
word 'design' needs to be read here in its original meaning of 'to
do or plan with a specific purpose in mind' (reading Jane Austen
might be a good refresher here). Let me emphasise here that a
purpose is different from a goal or an outcome. Purposes have
no end point, no final solution; they are an intention that can be
shared by others.

This is what makes a design approach so well suited to societal
issues: we know that when we work in a societal context, for
example a city like 's-Hertogenbosch, the designs of societies
are never finished. But what we can do is find as many
considerations and deliberations by as many stakeholders as
possible and try to find differences and synergies between them.
And if we group these stakeholders and the roles they play into
known categories, we will find something like Figure 55.

I define 'public space' (not to be confused with the public
domain) as the space shared by citizens, the market and
government. It is the space where their interests meet and need
to be served. Where their opinions may be conflicting but need
to be brought together in some kind of compromise. Where
we all have a role to play, based on our specific perspectives,
aspirations and concerns. In the diagram, I try to describe the
roles these stakeholders want to play in this public space. The
market wants to consciously design our experience of society, in
what we call service design. Government is (hopefully) pursuing
a vision of a society that is beneficial to all, inclusive and
acceptable, in cultural design. And citizens will bring their points
of view, their views, their interests, in what I call social design.
That is why I called social design a co-creative process between

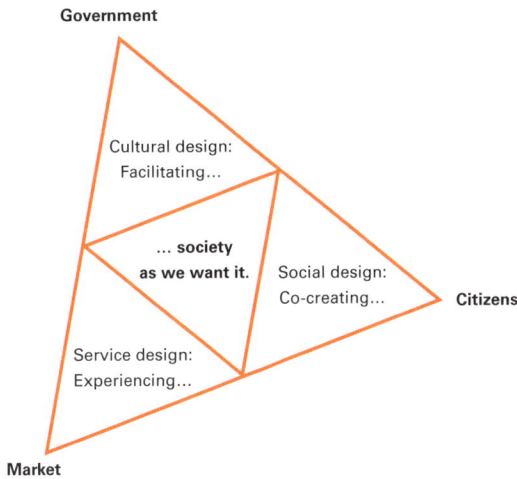

Government

Cultural design:
Facilitating...

... **society
as we want it.**

Social design:
Co-creating...

Citizens

Service design:
Experiencing...

Market

Figure 55.
Social
engineering in
public space.

stakeholders, which can be facilitated by the expertise of social designers. And the common goal of all these design approaches is society as we collectively want it to be. Governments will facilitate it, the market will create its experience, citizens will co-create this desired society. I call this process 'social engineering': the deliberate and purposeful interaction between different stakeholders and what they can bring to the table to move society forward.

Of course, 'designing a society' as such is not possible. In real life we have no idea what we want it to be. We have visions, views and positions, we have to face challenges, we have problems with its actual design, with each other's interests, and we will all have opinions about it all the time — only to find that our opinion is just one of many. Only to find that society is never 'finished', ideal, suitable for all.
Designing society is a continuous and dynamic process, a clash of cultures, visions and opinions that is constantly taking place in the public sphere. But at the same time, we still seem to know where we are going. The design of society we see before us is related to what we understand about ourselves. We have a

common idea of the right direction, or at least we are willing to discuss it. And that direction I would call identity.

When we look at 's-Hertogenbosch, we see a clear case of what origin and history can do (as in the case of Floriade and Val Gardena): it gives us a certain grip and understanding of things as they happen and develop. We evolve by looking backwards and forwards at the same time, in a continuous, interactive process of giving meaning to daily events and dialogues. We are constantly asking ourselves what things mean when they happen, how they relate to what we already know, where they might lead us and what we think about them. Once again, identity is an interactive concept, driven by both aspiration and descent. Drawing the line from where we came from to where we are now, and extending that line into the future, gives us a narrative about ourselves. It is our history in the making, our story into the future, our shared, tangible identity. And if we can stay true to that identity, we will know where to go.

Design thinking and identity
As I write this, the concept of 'design thinking' is hip and happening — and hijacked. Many people have been introduced to the concept of design thinking as a method, process or solution. You can take a one-day course in design thinking, and half the consultancies in the world offer it as an approach to solving organisational or strategic problems. But design thinking is not a method, process or solution — and it does not solve problems. It is a mindset. Design thinking is about opening up to possibilities, combining the views and knowledge of as many people as possible, letting go of assumptions, making room for the unexpected, playing around to see what happens... Design thinking is about asking questions about the status quo: why is this issue the way it is, what do we think about it, could it be different and would that be better, what can we learn from unexpected perspectives such as those of children, patients, other industries, other business models, and so on.

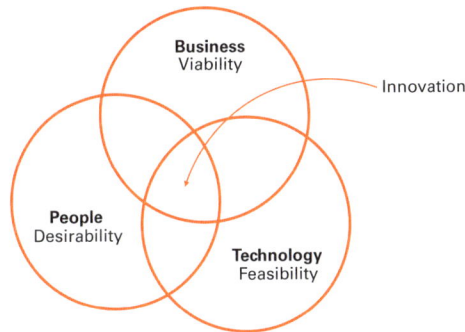

Figure 56.
Tim Brown's
representation
of the design
thinking
approach.

One of the early champions of design thinking was IDEO, a US-based design agency that aims for social impact in everything it does. As they say: 'We did not invent design thinking, but we want to play a major role in it'. In particular, it was IDEO leader Tim Brown who did much to spread the value and approach of design thinking (as a mindset!).

Brown created the model in Figure 56 based on the idea that design thinking serves innovation, a view with which I agree to the extent that innovation here can be anything. Originally the idea was that innovation comes from the right interaction between 'desirability', 'feasibility' and 'viability', or: do we want it, can it be done and does it create a viable business case? If you look at these three concepts, you will see that they are related to people, technology and business, in turn. The new idea behind this was the addition of the human perspective; we have been used to combining technology and business for a long time; but asking the question 'We can do this — but do we want to?' opens up a whole new perspective on innovation, ranging from morality to consequences and from personal needs to values.

What I find particularly interesting about this view is its appeal to what I called earlier the open mindset. A business case is a business case, and if it's not viable, we'll think again. Technology can be driven by needs and ambitions, but its availability is ultimately limited to what is physically possible. These are the hard, yes-or-no aspects of innovation. The human perspective, however, adds a soft aspect: what do we actually want? Why, or why not? And to what extent? How much of this innovation do we want, can we foresee and bear its consequences, what will it bring us, does it fit with our values, and so on. There is no 'yes' or 'no' here. And above all: there is no 'obsession' with a prescribed solution; from our human considerations we may agree to a certain direction, but no more than that.

When I tried to take Brown's idea to a more strategic level, I wondered if it would be useful to take the next step from describing design thinking as such. First of all, I wondered what kind of innovation was meant, and why Brown only saw it in the intersection of all three perspectives. I found more elaborate examples of the model that actually named these crossover types of innovation.[23] These versions depicted the central crossover as the experience as such; but if innovations are indeed adding up in the middle segment, this experience will be no less innovative and will reflect immersive, powerful new concepts. This is why this central part is usually called 'experience innovation'. This innovation is then supported by 'functional innovation' at the crossover between technology and people (after all, technology is supposed to make our lives easier and richer), 'process innovation' between technology and business (how do we organise ourselves for new concepts?), and 'emotional innovation' between people and business (in the area where we both try to give meaning to things).

Based on this version, I then tried to work the other way round, describing the three domains in 'thinking' terms at a strategic level. If we look at the business domain at a strategic level, we will take an analytical view. Technology will give us a synergetic approach to strategy. And the human perspective will add

Note 23.
The sources of these more elaborated versions are not really clear, as some authors attribute them to IDEO itself, others to third parties.

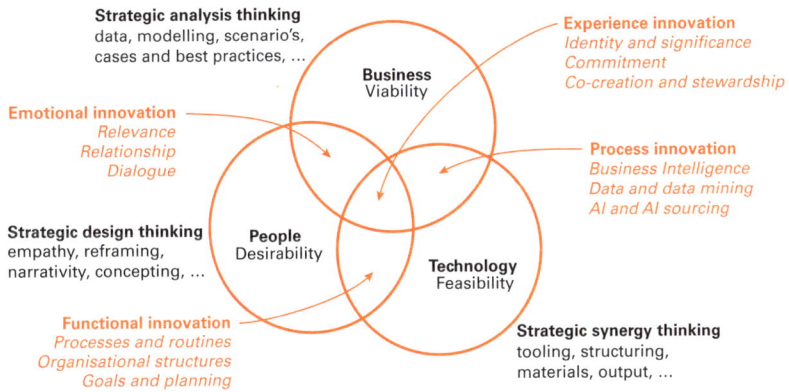

Strategic analysis thinking
data, modelling, scenario's,
cases and best practices, ...

Experience innovation
Identity and significance
Commitment
Co-creation and stewardship

Business
Viability

Emotional innovation
Relevance
Relationship
Dialogue

Process innovation
Business Intelligence
Data and data mining
AI and AI sourcing

Strategic design thinking
empathy, reframing,
narrativity, concepting, ...

People
Desirability

Technology
Feasibility

Functional innovation
Processes and routines
Organisational structures
Goals and planning

Strategic synergy thinking
tooling, structuring,
materials, output, ...

'design' (in Jane Austen's sense of the word). The worlds of strategic analysis and strategic synergy are well known and use familiar tools such as data, modelling, scenarios, cases and best practices to develop business strategies, and tools, structures, materials and output requirements for technology strategies. As Strategic Design Thinking is a new perspective, we also find new approaches such as empathy research, reframing, narrativity and concept development.[24]

But what really got me thinking about this strategic version of the model is the characters I found for the different domains of innovation. Process innovation is based on data and data mining, business intelligence and, increasingly, AI and AI sourcing. Functional innovation is about processes and routines, organisational structures and goals and planning. And emotional innovation is, of course, very much marketing, based on dimensions such as relevance, relationships and dialogue. But it was at the heart of the model where I suddenly found familiar concepts: identity and meaning, engagement, co-creation and stewardship are the dimensions of our shared experience and its innovation. We engage, recognise and relate to business, technology and our human perspective at the same time, we co-create new experiences, we create meaning and find the identity of our new way of looking at things.

Figure 57.
My elaboration of Brown's model: strategic design thinking as a new addition to strategy.

Note 24.
It might just be that the misunderstandings about what design thinking actually is, come from this strategic level: for here, we might easily mistake these approaches with tools and methods.

Now, I thought, there is an interesting role for design thinking for strategy: the way it opens up to arguments about identity. If we look at the case of 's-Hertogenbosch from this perspective, we see exactly what it does: it makes room for the grey areas between yes and no, between politics and cognition, because it understands meaning and commitment in its dynamics: who do we ultimately want to be as a city, given our history, culture, challenges and needs? And how can everyone contribute? The Agenda that emerged from the project made exactly these connections, defining not only what could be done or would benefit the community as a whole, but also what each individual citizen of 's-Hertogenbosch wanted.

Project management and identity
This chapter is about engagement, or more precisely, what identity can do to engage people in developments. I define engagement in a somewhat stricter way than is usual these days; apart from interaction as such (which is the common concept in the online world), I also want to include the content of that interaction and the commitment to that content. Engagement, in this view, is something personal: it happens because the issues at hand are considered important.

In the course of the 's-Hertogenbosch project we encountered this 'version' of engagement many times: from the people we talked to on the street to the project group, and from the city council to the mayor: this city provokes strong feelings of attachment, strong opinions, lively discussions. In such cases it is important to stick to the plan, or rather to stick to the objectives of the plan.

But there's a difference between the plan and the result of the plan: the former has well-defined goals that can be followed and checked; but, as I said, a society is never finished and cannot have finite goals. This dilemma (if it is one) has more than once led to misunderstandings, for example in our presentations to the City Council. We had to manage expectations at different levels to convince everyone of the path we were taking.

How do you define a goal when there is no fixed destination? How do you describe something that, by its very nature, is dynamic and almost intangible? And how do you keep everyone 'on board', especially at times when you have to allow for uncertainty, ambiguity, detours, time and leeway, because that is what a design process, and especially an identity-related design process, demands?

First of all, you ask everyone to trust the process. From the very beginning, during the pitch, we made it very clear that what we were proposing was not a clear-cut, mono-directional, efficient, goal-oriented approach. We said bluntly that if that was what the council wanted, they should hire someone else; but if they shared our belief in the need for a comprehensive and creative process, including empathic research, design steps and an identity-related approach, they would hire experts through us and end up with a much more valuable result. Apparently this was convincing, as we won the contract (and TwynstraGudde's very good reputation must have helped), but even during the project we had to come back to this point from time to time and explicitly ask everyone to trust the process we were following.

At the same time, we knew that our 'hidden' role was to understand and deal with the doubts that arose from time to time, because they were perfectly understandable from the point of view of a civil servant or a politician. So we not only asked for trust, we also made the process very clear. You have already seen the schematic of the project approach in the case description, but on the 'other side' we also used one of the 'canvases' developed by TwynstraGudde.
Based on the 'canvas thinking' of Alex Osterwalder c.s.,[25] the firm had developed, among other things, a 'programme canvas' and a 'project canvas'. These canvases were used extensively

Note 25.
Osterwalder and
Pigneur, 2010.

Opportunities	Context	Ambition	Cause	Unwanted effects
- Getting input and building a network for other processes - Better contacts between board and citizens	- Complementary to political cycle - Citizen's participation is on agenda - 's-H is evolving, whereto?	- Fully open conversation about the city's future - Develop unambiguous vision - Lasting community	- Is initiative of mayor - Need for better contact with citizens	- Exclude groups or insights - Substitution of existing interactions
Threats - Resistance of council and municipal organisation for feeling 'sidelined'	**Approach** - Empathy research by interviews - Discovering dilemma's, discussing dilemma's, mirroring image	**Objectives** - More support and involvement - More clarity on future - More inspired articulation of future	**Stakeholders** - Residents and entrepreneurs of 's-H - Municipal organisation - Other authorities and chain partners	
				Delimitation - No concrete policy - Not about other running initiatives
Preconditions - Fits withing existing policies - Fits within legal participation framework	**Efforts** - Round of interviews - Structured discussion - Articulating results	**Benefits** - X residents in community - 10 identified dilemma's - Visible movement on issues	**Results** - Conversation programme - Data research - Intermediate and final documents	

Resources	Organisation
- Municipal staff - Fixed budget for programme - Support by TwynstraGudde is budgeted	- Municipality core team, supported by external experts in programme set-up

in the often multi-year projects and programmes carried out by the consultants. Their strength is that they not only allow the elements of the project or programme to be analysed, organised and discussed, but also provide a common ground and reference during the implementation of the project or programme. We created a programme canvas for the 's-Hertogenbosch project (see Figure 58).

I do not want to go into too much detail here,[26] and will limit myself to explaining briefly that the nine central areas are the description of the actual programme, and the surrounding areas are the 'checks and balances' that make this programme resilient. What I want to look at here is the way in which 'ambition', 'targets' and 'benefits' are defined.

As you can see, we defined a multilateral ambition: not so much the agenda as such, but its character and its societal support and consequences. We aimed for a 'fully open conversation about

Note 25.
Osterwalder and Pigneur, 2010.

Note 26.
For a more in-depth description of this Canvas, see the book (in Dutch) on Program Management by Jos Bos c.s. in the Bibliography.

Figure 58.
Program Canvas for the 's-Hertogen-bosch programme.

the future of the city', a 'clear and widely supported vision of that future' and an 'enduring 'community' or movement of citizens'. This is where the somewhat intangible nature of the project's outcome becomes apparent.

Under 'Objectives' we have managed to state objectives that could describe an outcome with an open end. Again, society does not allow for an end point, so what were we trying to achieve? We described the objectives as improvements to the current situation: 'more support and involvement', 'more clarity about the future of 's-Hertogenbosch' and 'a more inspired articulation of that future'. This is where we started to touch on the identity aspects of the city. We then summarised the return on these three objectives in 'Benefits': 'X number of residents permanently involved in a community', '10 identified dilemmas of the city' and 'Visible movement on a number of issues'. We agreed that this was not a bad way of describing the results of a social programme.

Running a project or programme on identity issues will always have this aspect of uncertainty. When we talk about our identity, to some extent we don't know what we are talking about. We can find metaphors, approximations, stories and ambitions, but identity will remain intangible, precisely because of its dynamic and interactive nature. What I consider to be the identity of the city has a lot to do with my own identity.
Fortunately, describing the city's identity was not the task here (and we would have taken a very different approach if it had been); engaging with the city's identity was. And in the case of 's-Hertogenbosch, we found that this identity was very close to people's hearts and souls; and that engagement with it was therefore within reach. As long as we made it clear why, with what and how we wanted to develop this engagement. Again, being very clear about what you are going to do and why helps when you are entering an intangible domain such as identity and its perception.

If we want to find authentic answers, we need authentic commitment.

Understanding values and drivers of people will make you understand their questions.

For real engagement, be patient and keep your back straight.

We always need multiple perspectives to be successful.

Working on intangible themes asks for ultra clear processes.

Definition issue VII: social identity

Identity and ownership

Identities have no owner. I am not the owner of my character, values and assumptions; I more or less experience them as given. And community identities are no exception here, since they are established by the interaction between members of the community in time.
But social identity is in many cases certainly more visible than its individual or personal pendant. Communities more explicitly express the constituting values of their identity. These values are shared between the individual and the group, or the other way around: the community established itself by attracting persons with the same values. And this explicitness might almost be confused with ownership.

The process of reflecting on yourself.

Understanding and expressing your identity.

The Netherlands Social Childcare Association goes into depth.

Scenarios and strategic options, imagination and expression, sensemaking and sensegiving.

Epilogue

Reflecting on yourself.

Becoming who you already are.

The 'second feminist wave' of the 1960s and 1970s encouraged women to enter the labour market on a large scale. Well-maintained childcare facilities were seen as an important prerequisite for this. Today, almost half of all children in the Netherlands attend childcare two or three times a week, a figure that has almost doubled since around 2005. This may look very impressive, but at the same time most children in the Netherlands go to childcare for relatively few hours a week, most parents work part-time and share the care of their children between them, and there are some alternatives such as 'host parents', informal care by family and some self-organised networks of friends.

The childcare sector is under considerable pressure. Demand outstrips supply, the cost model has long been rather unclear (and is still under discussion, see below), which creates a need for efficiency and effective business models, the labour market is tight (especially in the social sectors in the Netherlands) and quality demands are high, which of course adds to the pressure. The response of providers in the sector has long been to scale up in order to meet these challenges; the number of providers has decreased significantly, while the number of 'child places' has increased.

There is one aspect of the organisation of the childcare sector in the Netherlands that is particularly relevant from an identity perspective: the fact that about half of the childcare places are provided by for-profit companies and the other half by not-for-profit companies. Childcare obviously offers a good profit model, judging by the amount of private equity invested in the sector. Of course, there would be nothing wrong with this if we did not also have a large amount of public funding in the sector. The Dutch government subsidises childcare for young children, mainly for emancipatory and educational reasons. At the moment, the government is even discussing the possibility of making childcare almost free for everyone. All in all, however,

212 | Becoming who you already are

this means that some public money is going into the pockets of private investors — which of course leads to discussions in the sector and in society as a whole.

This discussion goes beyond the mere fact that (mostly foreign) private investors make money from Dutch public money spent on childcare; we are also experiencing different choices in the two parts of the sector. Childcare is needed everywhere, not only where people can afford it, but perhaps even more so where they cannot.

This means that in areas where the earning conditions for childcare providers are more difficult (such as low-income urban areas or low-density rural areas), there is less profit to be made from setting up and maintaining a childcare centre. The fear is that the for-profit part of the sector will stay away from the less profitable business cases and pass the costs on to the not-for-profit part, which is more socially oriented.

The main reason for encouraging the use of childcare is educational. Research shows (as does gut feeling) that children who are used to being part of a group from an early age grow up with stronger social and emotional skills and are better able to sustain themselves later in life. Being the sole object of attention at home is of course very important — but so is understanding that the world does not revolve entirely around you. In addition, social skills such as conversation, negotiation, understanding and balancing people's interests, and awareness of different cultures and ways of looking at life are easy for children to pick up, and helping them to do this from the start gives them a head start in life. Special attention and rights are given to children at risk of disadvantage, who benefit spectacularly from participation in peer groups at a very young age.

In short, there is a very social aspect to childcare, which is the main reason why the government encourages its use.[27] And it is believed that the socially oriented foundations and associations

Note 27.
Since at this time we experience quite severe labour scarcity in The Netherlands, the stimulus on participation in the labour market by young parents that comes from childcare possibilities of course has great importance.

that form the non-profit part of the sector will invest more in this aspect than their profit-oriented colleagues, for whom cost is a more important argument.

The views I am expressing here on the disadvantages and risks of profit-oriented childcare come from the Dutch Association for Social Childcare (Branchevereniging Maatschappelijke Kinderopvang or BMK). About two thirds of the non-profit organisations (mostly foundations) in the healthcare sector are members of this association, which means that about 200,000 childcare places at almost 5,000 locations are represented by the BMK. Typically, members are medium-sized to large organisations.

Although the BMK values its social character, it has been somewhat reluctant to emphasise these social aspects in its participation in the public debate on the organisation of childcare in the Netherlands. The political and social interests of the profit and non-profit organisations are largely the same, which means that the associations of these organisations often form partnerships. They need each other in order to present a representative stance. However, the arguments they use to support their positions are different. To give an example, the concept of quality in profit-making organisations is understood as a certain level of compliance with standards that guarantee the best offer to parents; in social childcare, 'quality' tends to have a more substantive meaning, addressing issues of well-being, social behaviour and preparing children for life, but also the pedagogical and didactic quality of the staff, which requires good training, coaching, and so on. Participating in the social debate has therefore been a balancing act between avoiding sensitivities and being firm in our positions.

The question was whether this balancing act influenced the discussion and thus the interests of the association's members. Or as I would put it from my identity perspective: to what

extent it made the character, profile, position and proposal of the BMK visible or invisible. Having a strong profile will inevitably make you a stronger discussion partner, but the question is whether, in this case, this would also benefit the BMK's positions.

I was asked to support the reflection process on this issue in 2021, and the BMK and I worked together for almost a year. Precisely because of the doubts about the effects of a stronger profile, we chose an investigative approach in which we would be able to compare choices and options. This makes our collaboration an interesting case to tell about the process of self-reflection that is inevitable when trying to make one's identity explicit.

The first step we took was to consult widely with the association's members. As we were in the aftermath of the COVID-19 pandemic in 2021, we decided to hold online sessions with about 50 people from the member organisations and some chain partners and stakeholders. We discovered that the work and interests of the BMK touch on three areas: politics and policy-making ('Who decides on the direction of development?'),

Figure 59.
Positioning social childcare: the BMK members' inventory of stakeholders in the policy, proposition and organisation domains, varying from public healthcare to schools and from governments to parents.

Gemeenten

Onderwijs

Ouders

Jeugdzorg

Domein Welzijn

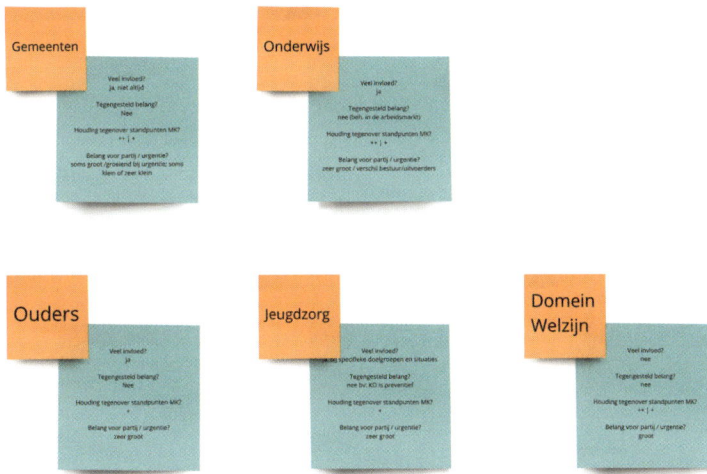

organisation ('Who takes care that things actually work?') and proposition ('Who do we work for?'). The BMK connects these three domains from a childcare perspective. We then mapped the stakeholders, partners and other actors in these domains and found a motley collection of governments, public and private actors and other domains such as sport or youth care.

We noticed that the practice of implementation was being looked at particularly closely: stakeholders in policy-making or vision-development were always seen at a greater distance by this group than stakeholders working with them in this practice. We assumed that this meant that vision and policy were likely to be seen as a central task of the BMK.
We completed our perspective on stakeholders by describing the positions and interests of the five most important ones: how big do we think their influence is, do we have conflicting interests, what is their view of BMK, how important are we to them? One of the interesting things we found here was that the for-profit part of childcare should be seen as a partner, not a (conflicting) stakeholder: in the broader perspective of the childcare sector, both players have a comparable position.

Figure 60.
Positioning social childcare: the five main stakeholders and their positions towards social childcare, according to the association's members: municipalities, education, parents, youth care and the domain of wellbeing.

Children
We offer children early development on a social, psychological and cognitive level; and therefore more equal opportunities for all children.

Parents
Together with parents, we offer support for their child's well-being and development (pedagogical partnership); furthermore, we offer parents the possibility of participation in social and economic life and the promise of 100% quality-oriented spending of their contribution.

Child professionals
We offer the other professionals working with and for children a strong and substantive chain partnership in the domain. We do so from a strong profile and in the form of interprofessional cooperation.

Employers, politics and policy and other stakeholders
We offer stakeholders early development and more opportunity for children, as well as a labour market stimulus, a prevention function, a 100% quality-oriented investment and our expertise. Finally, we are point of contact and cooperation partner in the domain.

Having found that we could see little difference between the for-profit and not-for-profit parts of childcare in terms of their positioning in the market, the next step was to describe the proposition of the social part of childcare to see if we could find more character differences there. By proposition we meant what we offer. Irreverently put: what could people 'buy' from us? And was this proposition the same for all our stakeholders? The group identified four audiences and therefore four propositions (Box 3).

In Chapter 6 on stakeholder management, I introduced the 'value cycle' model that I developed to describe the value proposition of sector associations, and which we naturally used in this reflection process. This time we used it to find the 'tasks' that emerged from the BMK's position and proposition. We distinguished between the tasks of the association (in yellow) and those of the members (in blue). Our main conclusion was

Box 3.
Social childcare sector propositions to the different stakeholders.

Figure 61.
Value Cycle-
based inventory
of sector and
association
assignments.

that the social part of the childcare sector needed a much stronger profile and position. If we really wanted to take a stand on the challenging aspects of our ambitions (such as 100% quality-led investment or equal opportunities for all children), we needed to be much more outspoken. And we found that most of the tasks were aimed at organising ourselves around that outspokenness.

As this 'outspokenness' emerged as one of the main challenges, we briefly explored the role of the BMK and its members in communication. We saw three possible models of communication here: the BMK as the spokesperson for the sector's positions, the members being enabled by the BMK to express these positions themselves, and the BMK as the centre

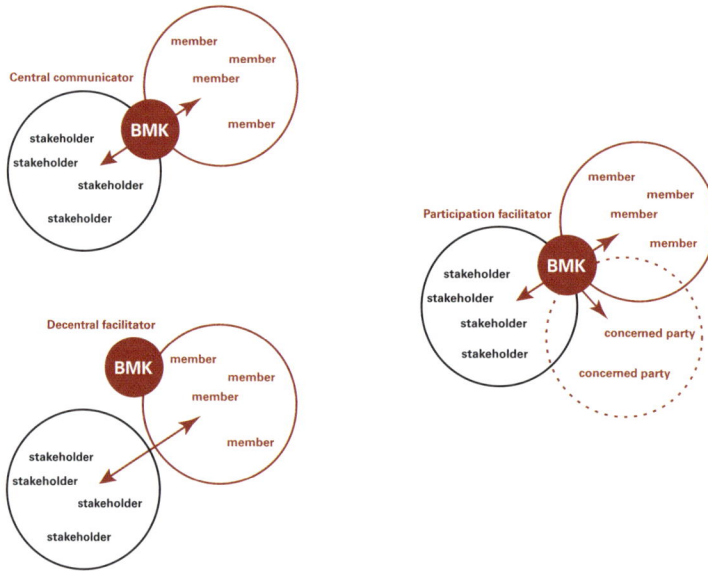

of a more or less participative process between members, chain partners and stakeholders, facilitating a dialogue in which positions are developed and shared. The discovery we made here was that these three models were in fact already being used simultaneously, depending on the issue and the communicative situation.

The final part of this consultation with members was to evaluate the four dimensions we had explored: how to measure the quality we wanted here and the progress we were making on them. We described four quality scales for positioning, proposition, organisation and communication, set values at the extremes of the axes and assessed where we wanted to be and where we actually were. We could then see what we needed to work on in our next steps.

After this round of consultation, we worked with the association's board as a working group and sounding board made up of members. Now that we had gathered broad input,

Figure 62. Communication modalities of the sector association: spokesperson, facilitator and participation platform.

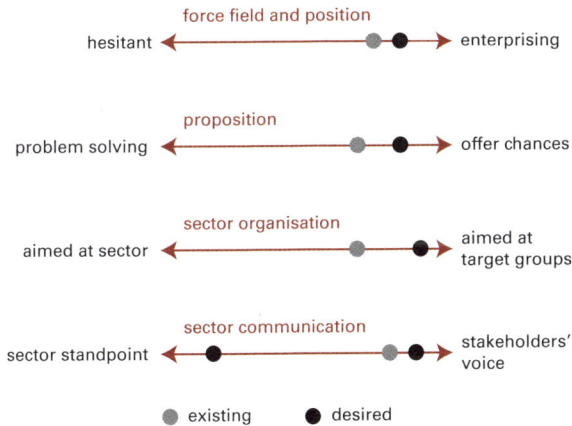

force field and position

hesitant ←——————●—●——→ enterprising

proposition

problem solving ←————————●—●——→ offer chances

sector organisation

aimed at sector ←—————————●——●—→ aimed at target groups

sector communication

sector standpoint ←——●———————●—●——→ stakeholders' voice

● existing   ● desired

Figure 63. Quality dimensions on position, proposition, sector organisation and communication, describing the actual and desired situation.

we needed to find direction and make choices — but have those choices tested. With this constellation of groups, we built in the right guarantees for that.

We began by analysing the results of the consultation and summarising them under three main themes: what should we work on? See Box 4 for the results. As you can see, we were pretty hard on ourselves: we really had to change things here. To make our change both understandable and open, we then defined three principles for the themes (Box 5). In this way we could follow common guidelines, but still be able to interpret what needed to be done in specific cases and situations.

The next step was to decide on the positioning and the communicative direction. The first thing we decided was that from now on we would no longer talk about the BMK as the spokesperson, but would present 'social childcare' as the spokesperson. After all, the BMK was there to facilitate this sector and its points of view, not the other way round. It also

Theme 1: strength of position
It is becoming clear, also through the results of the past period, that formulating and propagating a clear and unambiguous position, both by the BMK and its members, works. Here, it is important to start from an independent position as much as possible: what does social childcare stand for?

Theme 2: vision development of the proposition
BMK has an explicitly different vision of what is on offer from its commercial professional brethren and policymakers: childcare does not solve a problem but offers opportunities. In the complexity of the force field, it is important to express this message in the simplest, and therefore position-taking way possible. In other words: not to strive too much for consensus, but where necessary not to shy away from confrontation.

Theme 3: professionalisation of the organisation
Especially when we look at the communication of the sector, the level differences are quite large. Moreover, there is a lack of sufficient regular bodies for organising the sector effectively. Think of task forces to focus on certain themes, the organisation of joint knowledge development (e.g. via a platform), regular consultations at the vision level, et cetera.

Principle 1: As a sector, we do only that, which is in the best interest of every child's opportunities.
This is the main distinction of social childcare from many of the parties working in the broad sector of childcare: every decision we make, we put against the bar of what it does for the child. In this way, we avoid going down improper paths.

Principle 2: Social childcare reasons from opportunities, not problems.
Rather than seeing ourselves as an economic facility, we see ourselves as a social stimulus: providing every child with a starting situation that gives it the same opportunities as everyone else, ensures that society as a whole also benefits.

Principle 3: The sector association does only that, which individual members cannot do.
Either we do it ourselves, because it is an emphatic focal point; or we facilitate members to do it. In either case, the trade association is providing a service to members.

Box 4.
Elaborations on the three dominant themes to work on: position, proposition and organisation.

Box 5.
Principles for our work on the themes: what will guide our decisions?

The Children's Union: the sector as an advocate for every child

The most obvious option is for the MKO to act as the expert and advocate for the young child's interests in society. In this option, the sector becomes, as it were, the Consumers' Association of childcare (with the BMK as its headquarters): from a critical and independent point of view, it monitors which developments affect childcare, what that does to the opportunities of each child, which standards can be developed for the quality of childcare, how, in short, the interests of each child are best protected and promoted.

Social childcare knows what is good for every child: in this option, the sector and the BMK become the substantive authority on childcare: the party that, better than anyone else, and from only one interest (that of every child) researches, fathoms and reports. 'Social childcare. The best for every child.'

The Children's Party: the sector as a political player

A step further would be for the sector to position itself more explicitly in the political arena and to represent its own sharp point of view. In this option, the sector takes an emphatic stand in the social arena, articulates critical positions and heads towards achieving political successes. The social-childcare sector is a political, one-issue party. The content, however much in the interest of the child or focused on quality, is ultimately subservient to the result achieved in the social debate: we are only there when we enforce something.

You cannot avoid the social-childcare sector: in this option, the sector and the BMK develop into a political authority on childcare: the party that represents, takes a stand, lobbies, negotiates and puts pressure. The day-to-day role of that action falls to the BMK, which in turn is fed by its members.
'Social childcare is there for every child.'

The Children's Community: the sector as a social platform

Still further would mean the sector developing into a mouthpiece and knowledge developer in terms of the interests of all stakeholders in childcare. Besides representing the interests of the stakeholders in childcare (children, parents, employers, social domain, municipalities, etc.), the sector here also becomes a knowledge developer; not by developing that knowledge itself, but by facilitating (with the BMK as contractor) a platform for the development of that knowledge. The sector as a community with an explicit interest: that of every child.

The social childcare sector is childcare: the sector and the BMK grow into a central authority for childcare, the place where the social debate takes place because everyone is committed to it, where steering takes place on the basis of substantive arguments rather than political ones, and where day by day the knowledge is developed that leads to a responsible model for childcare.
'Social childcare. A good start for every future.'

Box 6.
Three possible strategic positions for social childcare and the BMK.

Are we answering the question?	The advocate > Why. *The authority that knows what is right for every child.*	The political player > What. *The political authority you cannot ignore.*	The social platform > How. *The central authority: we are childcare.*
Strong position: Are we making clear what social childcare stands for?	We make our social character very clear here: what future are we preparing our children for?	We may assume our viewpoint is shared but are too action-oriented.	We can form a networking organisation but become dependent on the insights of participants.
Visionary proposition: Can we take a stand from our validated vision?	We put quality over profit and create a warm, social personality.	We become too organisational here and lose our substantiality.	We can connect and have a strong societal proposition but also become broad and instrumental.
Professional sector: Do we eliminate level gaps through coherence and joint knowledge development?	We use what we have at hand and can standardise.	We will be very able to share our vision on quality over profit here.	We also share knowledge amongst ourselves.

Are we following our principles?	The advocate > Why. *The authority that knows what is right for every child.*	The political player > What. *The political authority you cannot ignore.*	The social platform > How. *The central authority: we are childcare.*
As a sector, we do only what is in the best interest of the child's opportunities.	We make that very clear in this option: we always do everything for the child.	In this option, we are keen on those interests.	We can partner with any stakeholder. The position not strong because of dependency on 'participants', who may also bring in other interests.
Social childcare arges from opportunities, not problems.	Here, we put the future first (whichever it is) and show our social character.	The message here is: learning to live together is a must.	In this option, you have to know what you are talking about, and listen to those directly affected.
The sector association does only that, which individual members cannot do.	'BMK is there for us.' And we can standardise sector-wide.	Central role by the BMK; role of the members needs to be organised. But: playing politics is not a competence of childcare organisations.	We organise the social debate centrally, in which organisations can also contribute their knowledge and views.

made it possible to talk much more substantively about the sector's positions — not about interests, not about differences, but about the actual character and beliefs of the sector.
We used three strategic positioning options to enable our discussion (Box 6) and weighed these options against the insights we developed in the themes and the principles we defined earlier, using two matrices to ask ourselves whether we were responding to our challenges and following our principles (Figure 64).

In the end, we came to the conclusion that the third option would give us the best chance of taking a substantive stand,

Figure 64. Decision matrices, combining the possible strategic positions with the defined themes and principles.

which in turn would lead us to the open, strong position we were looking for. After all, we started with a question of visibility: how to become a more significant player in the childcare sector as a whole, and how to balance our ambition to have a social approach to childcare while still being able to work with the for-profit part of the sector. By choosing to promote a community in which children's interests are at the centre, we have been able to express our own character and at the same time be of value to any competing approach, not hesitating to gather and share lessons of value to all. After all, who can be against giving every future a good start?

In addition to these positioning choices, the end result of our collaboration consisted of a message house (pay-off, boilerplate, one-page and Q&A) and a communication strategy that could lead the BMK and the social childcare sector to the desired positioning. We stated that in everything the sector and the BMK communicated, the child as such should be at the centre, as the starting point of every message: 'We are the voice of the child'. And we decided to make a fundamental distinction between interactions at the collective level (to be taken care of by the BMK) and at the individual level (to be taken care of by the members), while at the same time, of course, these interactions should be consistent with each other — a responsibility given to the BMK to facilitate.

As a communication strategy, we decided to work with what we call a 'steady drumbeat': consistent, frequent repetition of the core messages at every opportunity, and a constant presence in the debate and dialogue, where the positions of the sector and the BMK are known in advance and interpreted for each specific situation. This kind of communication is very convincing, both for external stakeholders and for the internal target groups, in this case the members: we all know what we stand for. It is like 'positioning through communication' or 'strength through consistency'.

Identity aspects

As you can see, identity related processes are inevitably reflective in nature. You need to take a hard look at yourself to discover who you are at this time, for what reasons, and with what meaning to others, yesterday, today and tomorrow. This can be a rather confronting process for several reasons. Firstly, because you are asking questions that probe the deepest essence of who you are. You have to be completely honest with yourself, otherwise the whole thing is meaningless. And in doing so you will find some things that you may not like too much, ranging from weaknesses, blind spots and risks to real shortcomings, self-absorption and overestimation. On the other hand, you will also encounter your value, meaning and coherence; these are the more rewarding moments.

In order to break through the deadlocks and painful moments, as well as to expose assumptions (I will come back to this), the process needs to be respectful and challenging at the same time. We should not avoid our weaknesses in order to find our values and strengths. We are looking for our true self, in its beautiful and less beautiful aspects; if we are satisfied with the first thing we find, we may not get there. We have to dig deep. This is why identity projects need to take time and involve many people. We need to look and find, think and rethink, discover and reflect; we need our own honest views and perspectives and those of others; we need to ask what meaning we have or should have for our stakeholders, our partners and ourselves. And we need discussion — lots of discussion — to really discover what it all means.

Assumptions are one of the biggest risks in identity discovery. In everyday life we can hardly do without them. They bring clarity, perspective and order to the world around us. They help us stay on track because they rule out certain uncertainties. But when it comes to self-reflection, we need to realise that assumptions are nothing more than opinions, most of which are based on self-interest. We have to position our main competitor in some corner of the market, we have to assume that all our employees are loyal, we have to assess the importance of new technology for us in a limited way — or else we will all go mad. But as soon as we start to think about ourselves as an organisation, as a region, as a sector, we have to give up that luxury. Now we have to be honest, we have to examine the real situations, positions, meanings, otherwise we will not find ourselves, our real challenges and our real opportunities.[28] Now we will have to face the fact that some competitors are ahead of us, that not all employees are loyal, that we have missed out on a certain technology because it is the only way to take the next step.

The process I described for the BMK and the social childcare sector was no exception. We assumed that the for-profit part of the sector would be less sensitive to the interests of children and parents, only to find that this was not the case. We took for granted that all partners in the chain would know what we stood for — only to discover later that, to some extent, they did not. And we took it for granted that all members would have a comparable perspective on the meaning of the word 'social' — only to discover that we had some homework to do. But it was precisely through these sometimes painful discoveries that the BMK and the sector found the right way forward, the next steps and, above all, who they really wanted to be, i.e. what their ambitions were and how they should interact with their environment. In short, they discovered their identity.

Discovering your identity requires realism. 'This is who we really are right now, this is the meaning we have right now — are we happy with it? And if not, where do we want to go and how do we get there without losing ourselves?' So, in addition to realism, we also need the ability to be strong: to be honest and open with ourselves, to choose a realistic and comprehensible path of development, to dare to make choices and follow them through. At the same time, this strength is the best guarantee of your

Note 28.
My very esteemed colleague at TwynstraGudde, Rudy Kor, taught me to avoid assumptions by using a simple mnemonic called 'Anna', which translated to English would be 'Aana': Always Ask, Never Assume.

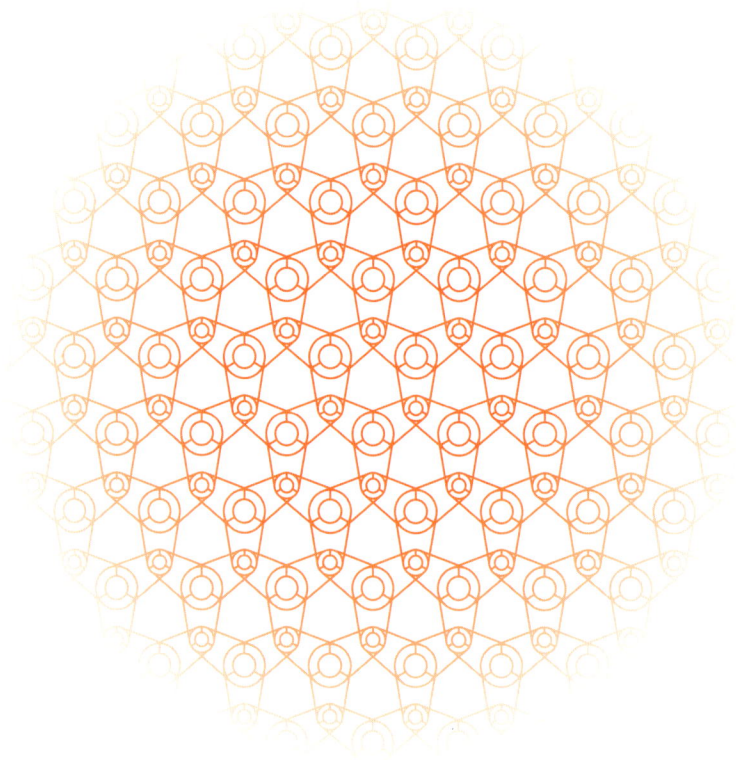

success. Let's take a look at an image from the first chapter (Figure 65). The image describes the reciprocity of identities: each identity must be perceived by an alterity that is also an identity in itself, making all identities essentially equal. We then discovered that by gaining some value for others, you can emerge from this grey maze and become a hub in the identity network. What you need for this is significance and a minimum number of moments in which this significance becomes visible. So if identity is about ambition and interaction, then showing your ambition and interacting with it will actually make you successful — it will make you a significant hub. And you will need the same courage and realism with which you went on

Figure 65.
The identity and
alterity network.

your journey of discovery in search of your true self. In the case of the BMK/social childcare sector, this is what we did with the considerations in the last two matrices (Figure 64), where we asked ourselves whether we were actually answering the question and whether we were following our principles; once again we see the balance and dilemma between interaction and consistency that is so typical of identity.

This may all seem like hard work, a painful and sobering process. But it is not. Done well, the search for your true self, without avoiding the challenges you are sure to encounter, can be very inspiring and a new beginning for your organisation, region or sector: your board and staff, your stakeholders and customers, your partners and investors. Done well, it will give you a beautiful, complete and inspiring view of yourself that can make you eager to get to work. You will see new opportunities, possible partnerships, satisfying results in front of you, precisely because you have gone through some loopholes; and of course, knowing yourself will make you stronger, more focused and more energetic; and therefore more significant, meaningful, valuable to others. This is what identity can do.

Scenario's for identity

You may have wondered where these three strategic positioning options for the social childcare sector came from. Of course, there is some intuition involved; but this book would not be complete without a description of a modelling exercise to capture and assess this intuition (which I also used as a background check in the case of the social childcare sector).

My former colleague Elisabeth Kroon and I co-authored a paper in 2008 on a scenario-based approach to positioning and profiling.[29] We started with an axis model in which relevant megatrends, trends and issues can be plotted according to their predictability and importance for the organisation, region or sector (Figure 66). The best way to do this is with a broad group

Note 29.
Kroon and Van Diemen, 2008.

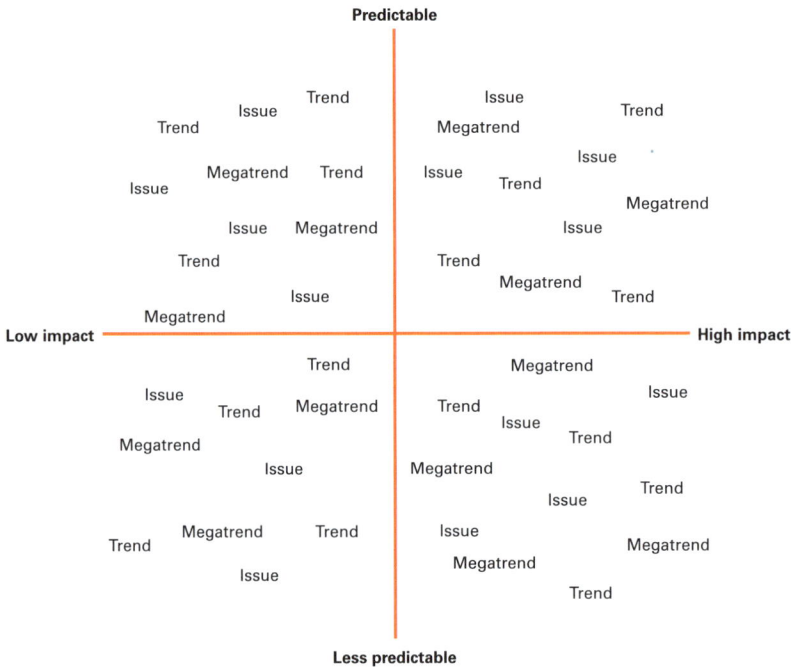

of stakeholders who can all shed light on what is happening in the world that is relevant to the organisation, region or sector, and to what extent. The trick is to gather as much information as possible and, through discussion, to put it all in the right place on the axis system.

This is a familiar way to start building scenarios, but Elisabeth and I added a twist that makes the approach interesting for positioning and profiling. In the predictable and high impact segment, the organisation (or region or sector) can choose its domain. After all, this segment should, by its very nature, be a familiar area for the organisation, its natural habitat, where it knows its place and role. So the choice of domain here should be quite obvious. The BMK and the social childcare sector chose 'growing attention to the social development of children' (without using the model, buy the

Figure 66.
Trendplot as a basis for a scenario-based positioning and profiling exercise.

way; as I said, I used this model in the background to get to the creation of strategic options later).

The unpredictable and high impact segment is where the organisation can choose its profile. This is where we start to talk about ambition: we want to have an impact on a particular trend or issue, an impact for which we will be known. This is where you take a stand. In the case of BMK, I thought that 'importance of knowledge sharing' was the trend they implicitly chose, because they were aiming for a profile of being an authority.

The next step is to construct a second system of axes, this time with the two trends or issues of choice and the range of extremes they may have. After all, we are talking about trends and issues that we do not know how they will develop, but they will develop within a certain range that can then be described. If we want to have an impact, we will try to influence this development, which essentially means that we will take a position within this system of axes.[30] For the social childcare sector, I have drawn the options that you can see in Figure 67.

The 'social development' axis ranges from the individual interest of each child to the collective interest of society — and we know that the emphasis will change all the time, depending on social and political discourses and events. I have drawn the axis of knowledge sharing from shared to co-created, because the openness of knowledge development is something that will be determined in practice.

We can now see four different pictures, depending on the development of the axes. If we start from the individual interest of the child and limit ourselves to the mutual exchange of knowledge, we would create a child advocate: someone who knows and defends the interest of the child. If we were to work from a collective perspective, we would become a political actor, defending the interests of children in society from our knowledge and position. We would create a platform for

Note 30.
People working with scenario planning will recognise the model as the basis of defining scenario's, and reproach me for mixing 'scenario's' with 'strategic options', and they are totally right. Yet, as I said, positioning and profiling yourself is about having an influence on developments, which is why I 'abuse' scenario's for the options to choose: where do we want to have an impact on the development of these two trends? You may hold me accountable for this creative use.

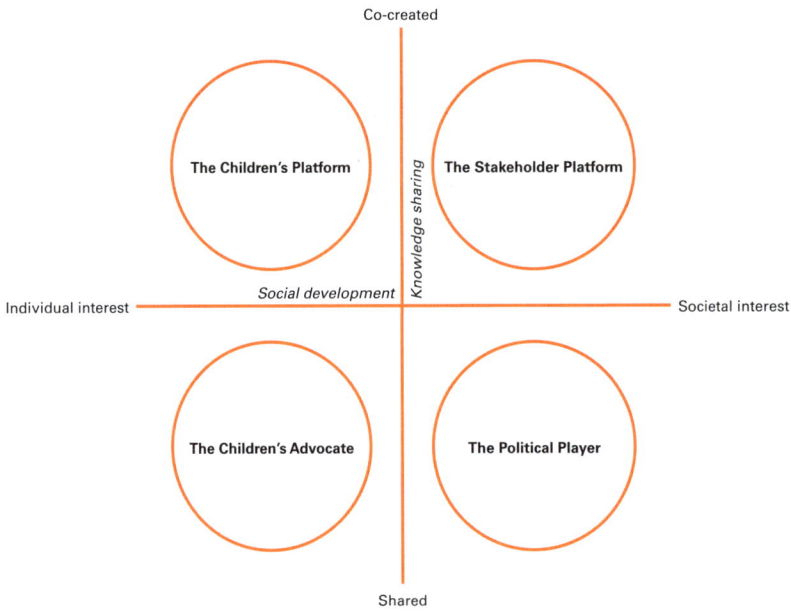

Figure 67.
Scenario-based positioning and profiling for the social childcare sector.

children's interests as soon as we start to co-create knowledge; and we would create a stakeholder platform if we were to do this from the collective perspective.

Since I was aware that the social child care sector saw the children's interest and the societal interest in social development as a continuum, I decided to combine the 'platform' options and create a 'societal platform' option here. I could not do the same for the advocate and political actor options because they would require very different roles for the sector and the BMK. So I ended up with three possible positioning options.

Showing new worlds

You will have noticed that there is a considerable amount of creativity involved even in laying strategic foundations such as positioning options. Imagining developments and their consequences, giving names and building images (in words and/or in pictures) of the 'futures' to choose from, making the not-yet-existent tangible and navigable, is essential to helping people make choices. Strategic choices are inherently abstract; but understanding their meaning for you and your future requires feeling, understanding, grasping: 'What are we choosing for when we choose a particular option?

I use a lot of storytelling, conceptualisation and imagery in my strategic work. I am always aware that we are talking about things that do not yet exist and are therefore difficult for most people to imagine. After all, working in an organisation, sector or region means that you know it as it is — not as it could be: What will my work, my responsibilities, my role be in the new situation? What does that mean on a day-to-day basis? How can I 'do' this role or responsibility? It is important to 'word' things, to find comparable examples, to make crossovers between now and the future, or to other sectors, to find pockets of the future in the present that people can recognise and strengthen in their understanding and conviction.

Being able to 'show' the new or hidden world we are aiming for is an indispensable part of the work. When we are discovering an identity, such as that of the social childcare sector and the BMK, making things comprehensible on more than a cognitive level will make people understand the significance of what we are discovering. And if it is done well, it will inspire them, make them want to do it. So I tend to name things at a more cognitive, sensory level ('The Children's Union', 'The Children's Party', and 'The Children's Community'), show imaginary examples of marketing campaigns, headquarters signatures, newspaper articles, or whatever helps to add a sense to what might be understood at a cognitive level, but is not yet persuasive. Because people deserve to be able to make a heartfelt choice.

Building commitment and coherence
A good description of what people in organisations experience when change is imposed on them is the 'sensemaking and

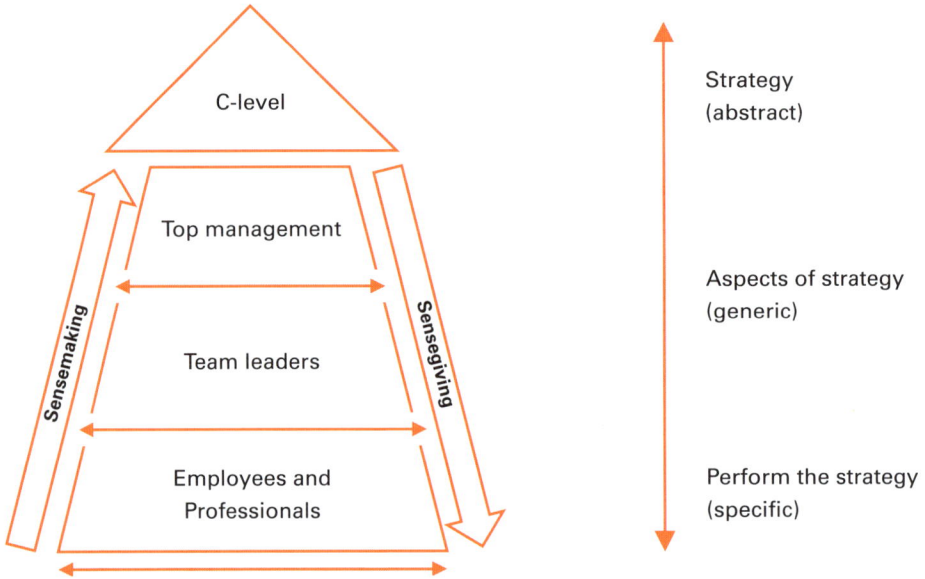

sensegiving' analysis by Gioia and Chittipeddi[31] in 1991. They describe the process of understanding the need for and nature of change in organisations by looking at the top-down and bottom-up directions of that change. When asked to change, 'sensemaking' is the bottom-up process in which people search for meaning: they try to understand the nature of the intended change. Sensegiving' is the top-down process of trying to influence this sensemaking and steer it in the desired direction of change. In other words, management will give sense to the desired change, people in the organisation will try to make sense of it. A version of this process described by my former TwynstraGudde colleague Sander Merkus looks like Figure 68.

Although this model of thinking about the process focuses on strategic change, it is also very valuable in supporting the acceptance and appropriation of other strategic concepts — such

Note 31.
Gioia and Chittipeddi, 1991.

Figure 68.
Sander Merkus' representation of sensegiving and sensemaking dynamics in an organisation.

as discovering and describing one's identity. In the case of the social childcare sector and the BMK, understanding what it means to be the social platform, the 'Children's Community', is both a top-down and a bottom-up process. The BMK board will try to explain the why, how and what of the choice they have made. Professionals working in the sector will discuss among themselves and with others what this means for them, both in day-to-day practice and at the tactical level of decision making for their own organisations. This discussion and its consequences will in turn be seen and understood by the BMK board, who will then be able to judge whether they have been clear enough, whether people have accepted and embraced the vision, and whether they are starting to implement it.

What we see here is the process of exchanging meanings throughout the hierarchy of, in this case, a sector. You will remember that we started the whole process of reflection with a broad consultation of the members; in other words, we started from the beginning with an exchange of visions and ambitions. And this exchange can be continuously monitored and managed: do we understand each other? Are we moving in the right direction? Do we see inspiring examples that we can use to engage others? Do we need to take corrective action? And so on.

Again, inspiration is a powerful element. If we can make people feel the benefits and the beauty of a vision for ourselves, for our importance as a sector, region or organisation, they will become proud, eager and inspired to fulfil that vision, to make it meaningful. They will show ambition and begin to act on that ambition. In short, they will live the identity.

Design principles for reflection

We need to be respectful and challenging at the same time.

Assumptions can be very tempting.

Accepting that you only discover what you already knew can be hard but has great value.

If lost, look for what makes you meaningful.

Inspiration asks for honesty.

Definition issue VIII: on definitions

You will have seen throughout this book that I carefully
avoided describing identity processes as 'definitions'. There is
nothing to define when it comes to identity, for the simple fact
that it is always already there. Looking for your identity means
to discover who you are, gain consciousness of yourself, make
your identity explicit.
I defined the concept of identity as ambition, interaction,
character, personality, all at the same time; those are the
things you can look for, which you can describe and make
tangible. Identity itself will then emerge as your more or less
hidden treasure, as something which presence you may have
suspected but were unable to express.
I think working on identity has fascinated me for so long
exactly for this aspect. We are like Michelangelo: we cut
away the excess marble to discover the image, beauty and
significance hidden inside the block. The balance between
respect and boldness, between being challenging and keep
listening and observing in identity work is something that
will never tire me. It leads to beautiful, significant and often
gratifying moments. It is these moments I wish to all of you.

Acknowledgements

This book could not have been written without the contributions and opinions of the people I have met in my professional and personal life.

First and foremost, there are my clients. The ones who gave me their trust to reflect and work on their challenges and development. Sometimes in short projects or not even beyond the pitch. Sometimes in relationships that have lasted for years. In all cases, they have given me the opportunity to develop my own thoughts on identity by studying their specific situation and challenges. There are simply too many to mention; some of them appear in the cases in this book. But to all of them I express my deepest gratitude.

Thanks to all the people who looked at the cases in this book and gave their permission. Thanks to Maria and Ingeborg for going through the manuscript of this book and coming up with so many suggestions for improvement. Thank you, Maarten, for another amazing picture. And thanks to Harm van Kessel of BIS Publishers for believing in me and supporting my efforts.

Then there are the many friends, colleagues and collaborators in my professional career, without whom this book would never have been written. During my time at Plano, my work at Tel Design and Filmac, my long track at Total Identity and my years at TwynstraGudde and most recently at Metacy and Stijn van Diemen Strategy, I met hundreds of dedicated, inspiring people who were willing to show me the way, support my efforts and development and inspire me every day. Un gracias especial a la gente con que tuve la suerte de colaborar durante mis estancias en España. And special thanks to Annemarie van Noort, the best project manager in the world, to Manfred Roosenstein†, my very loyal companion when it came to conquering the market, to

Renaat van Cauwenberge, who made me understand the very peculiar aspects of the Flemish market, y al inolvidable Paco Bascuñán† por enseñar y explicarme su trayecto tan individual. All of you: thank you for being there, working with me and teaching me so much.

Two people in my professional life have been of particular importance to me, and this book would never have been written without our many years of collaboration: Edwin van Praet and Hans Paul Brandt.

Edwin is a brilliant designer of corporate identity and editorial design. He has been my designing right hand for almost twenty years. I cannot remember any moment in our collaboration that we agreed upon any subject — and exactly because of that, Edwin managed to sharpen and shape my thoughts each and every time, urging me to be explicit and asking me what, in my opinion, was the bare essence of the project at hand — 'otherwise I cannot design it.' Thank you so much for bearing with me Ed. And thank you for time and again creating these beautiful answers to the impossible questions I came up with; many of those answers are in this book.

Hans was CEO of the design agency with the world-famous name Total Design when, in 2000, he decided to rename it Total Identity. This immediately caught my attention: it was the first time that I realised that the concept of identity was indeed very powerful. When Hans and I met for the first time in 2003 and he asked me to direct the The Hague office of Total Identity, it was the beginning of a lifelong relationship in which we have worked and continue to work together in various constellations. Many of the models you will find in this book are the result of our discussions. Thank you, Hans, for your inspiration and loyalty.

But the most important people in my life are, of course, my family and close friends. My loving and lovely wife Ingeborg, who gave me the space to write this book and who supported and supports me in every way. My dear friends, who inspire me and sharpen my thoughts every time we meet or talk. And my dear Jolient, who has been the centre of my life for more than twenty years and has never stopped pushing me forward.

I dedicate this book to my two sons, Bram and Guus, who make me proud every day as they develop, find their role in this world, discover their own identities and inspire me in their wake.
You have asked me more than once what my work is about — well, this is it.

Leiden / L'Eliana, January 2025.

Credits and consents

I asked for consent on the cases wherever I could. But some of these cases are a bit older, and the people who were working with me at the time may have left or taken up other responsibilities. I did have all cases checked by people who were included, if not as a commissioner, then as least as a colleague or partner, and asked for permission by clients and agencies wherever that was still possible. I apologise for any mistakes or gaps in my efforts. Please contact me if you feel I have overlooked you.

Case credits
These descriptions of who were involved in the cases in this book are deliberately far from complete. I decided to list only core project teams and clients to avoid long, tedious lists. The agencies I mention describe my personal connection to the project or commissioner; in many cases, other agencies and professionals were also included.

Floriade World Expo 2022 (Total Identity, 2011-2012)
Client: Municipality of Boskoop / Province of South Holland
Core team: Ron Kervezee (Boskoop), Cor Geense (pZH), Marleen Maarleveld (Arcadis), Klaas Hofman (OMA), Hans Paul Brandt (Total Identity Amsterdam), Edwin van Praet, Stijn van Diemen (Total Public)

Vlaamse Instelling voor Technologisch Onderzoek (VITO)
(Total Identity , 2016-2018)
Client: VITO
Core team: Kristin Geboers (VITO), Renaat van Cauwenberge (Total Identity Antwerp), Edwin van Praet, Stijn van Diemen (Total Public)

Tergooi (Total Public, 2012-2017)
Client: Tergooiziekenhuizen / Tergooi
Core team: Lucielle Praktiek, Marieke Quant, Ruurd Jan Roorda,
(Tergooi), Annemarie van Noort, Edwin van Praet, Stijn van
Diemen (Total Public)

Gardena-Gröden (Total Identity, 2007-2008)
Client: Saslong Classic Club / FIS Ski World Cup Organising
Committee
Core team: Stefania Demetz, Gernot Mussner (Saslong Classic
Club), Manuel Demetz, Wilco Lensink, Stefano Baldini (Total
Identity Italy), Edwin van Praet, Stijn van Diemen (Total Identity
The Hague)

Maester (Creative Capital Studio and Metacy, 2020-2021)
Client: Maester
Core team: Tim van Pappelendam, Nina Goedknegt, Sophie
Hamann (Maester), Ron van Bijsterveld, Hans Paul Brandt, Stijn
van Diemen, Dirk Laucke (Creative Capital Studio and Metacy)

National Healthcare Association (Total Public)
Core team: Annemarie van Noort, Edwin van Praet, Stijn van
Diemen (Total Public)

's-Hertogenbosch (TwynstraGudde, 2019-2020)
Client: Municipality of 's-Hertogenbosch
Core team: Sander de Vuyst, Gertie Korevaar, Jack Mikkers
('s-Hertogenbosch), Iris van Genuchten, Sterre Casier, Stijn van
Diemen (TwynstraGudde)

BMK (Metacy/Stijn van Diemen Strategy, 2021-2025)
Client: Branchevereniging Maatschappelijke Kinderopvang (BMK)
Core team: Hélène Smid, Loes Ypma (BMK), Stijn van Diemen
(Metacy/Stijn van Diemen Strategy)

Photo and illustration credits

I did everything in my power to find and name all the credits for illustrations, methods and publications I used in this book. If anyone should feel that I did not honour his or her work as I should have — please let me know, so I can correct eventual errors.

Page 18: Floriade brand as presented in the bidbook.
Figures 1 to 4: from the Floriade bidbook. 1 and 4 created by OMA.
Figure 5: Birkigt et al, 1994, p. 23.
Figure 6: from Van Diemen (2005).
Page 40: image from VITO's corporate presentation.
Figure 7: workshop result.
Figures 8, 9: workshop results.
Figure 10: concept work.
Figure 11: Brand Compass co-created by Total Identity.
Page 57: concept work.
Page 63: image from introduction campaign of Tergooi brand.
Figure 12: Tergooi basic and introduction campaign elements; Proposition model from 2013 Multiannual strategic plan.
Figure 13: images from Tergooi internal communication; photography from 'Zorgen', Tergooi corporate movie created by Corb!no.
Figure 14: Health Studio corporate brochure cover and screen captures form broadcasts.
Figure 15, 16: images from Tergooi internal communication.
Figure 17: image from Alrijne internal communication.
Figure 18: From Glijn and Van Diemen (2008).
Figure 19: basic model from Van der Houwen (2007); completed model from workshop result.
Figure 20: original image created by Renaat van Cauwenberge, Total Identity Antwerpen.
Figure 21: from Tergooi visual identity manual.
Figure 22: images from Tergooi internal communication.
Page 93: top and middel image by author; bottom imnage by Johnny Africa (Unsplash)
Figure 23: workshop result.
Figure 24: corporate story written by Manuel Demetz (Total Identity Italy) and Gernot Mussner (Saslong Classic Club).
Figure 25: from the GardenaGroeden design manual.
Figures 26, 27: by the author.
Figure 28: this version drafted by Hans Paul Brandt and Martijn Kagenaar, Total Identity.
Figure 29: workshop result.
Figure 30: design result.
Figure 31: from De Heus and Berkhout (2009), adapted by author.
Figure 32: author's collection.
Page 122: screen image by Dirk Laucke.
Figure 33 to 35: workshop results and marketing manual.
Figure 36: Treacy and Wiersema (1995), p. 45.
Figure 37,38: by author.
Figure 39: Brandt and Van Moorsel (2010), adapted by author.
Figure 40: by author.

Page 154: Gadina on Pixabay, adapted by author.
Figure 41: by author.
Figures 41 to 44: workshop results. Photography by Pixabay and Christian Buehner, Fred Moon and Barna Bantis (Unsplash).
Figures 45 to 49: by author.
Figure 50: results consolidation of image scan research for the Netherlands Senate, carried out by author in 2013.
Page 180: photographer unknown / project team.
Figure 51: left photo unknown, right photo by Marc Bolsius for Brabants Dagblad.
Figure 52: from the project proposal document.
Figure 53: photographer unknown / project team.
Figure 54: project results.
Figure 55: by author.
Figure 56: IDEO / Tim Brown.
Figure 57: author's adaptation of design thinking model by Tim Brown.
Figure 58: model from Bos et al (2018), project document.
Page 210: Piyapong89 on Pixabay.
Figure 59 to 64: workshop results.
Figure 65: from Van Diemen (2005).
Figure 66: from Kroon and Van Diemen (2008).
Figure 67: project result by author.
Figure 68: this representation delivered to me by Sander Merkus PhD.
Author's photo, page 247: Corb!no/Maarten Corbijn.

Bibliography

These are some of the publications that shaped my thinking. Sometimes they were an inspiration. Sometimes they were a reference work. Sometimes they changed my insights. Sometimes I wrote them myself. In any way, if you're interested, here's some more to read on the subject of identity.

Bascuñán, Paco and Diemen, Stijn van (2007): *Interactie | Interacción.* Total Identity.

Baumann, Zygmunt (2007): *Liquid Times; Living in an Age of Uncertainty.* Cambridge.

Bettonville, Ellen and Diemen, Stijn van (2015): *Here we are; Over de kracht van het verschil.* Total Identity.

Bierut, Michael and Hall, Peter (1998): *Tibor Kalman: Perverse Optimist.* Booth-Clibborn Editions.

Birkigt, K., Stadler, M. M., & Funk, H. J. (Eds.). (1994): *Corporate Identity: Grundlagen, Funktionen, Fallbeispiele* (7th ed.). moderne industrie.

Bos, Jo, Prevaas, Björn, Stoop, Helmuth (2018): *Leiderschap van de programmamanager; Hoe jij het verschil maakt in doelgerichte opgaven.* Boom.

Brandt, Hans Paul and Bügel, Jurjen (2003): *Een seconde voor de werkelijkheid.* Total Identity.

Brandt, Hans Paul and Bügel, Jurjen (2005): *Van merkpropositie naar betrokkenheid en dialoog.* Total Identity.

Brandt, Hans Paul and Moorst, Annemiek van (2010): *The customer is king; Value creation in the service economy.* Total Identity.

Caluwé, Leon de and Vermaak, Hans (2006): *Leren veranderen; Een handboek voor de veranderkundige* (2nd ed.). Kluwer.

Castells, Manuel (2009): *The Rise of the Network Society, The Information Age: Economy, Society and Culture Vol. I* (2nd ed.). Blackwell.

Castells, Manuel (2009): *The Power of Identity, The Information Age: Economy, Society and Culture Vol. II* (2nd ed.). Blackwell.

Castells, Manuel (2010): *End of Millennium, The Information Age: Economy, Society and Culture Vol. III* (2nd ed.). Blackwell.

Castells, Manuel (2009): *Communication Power.* OUP.

Demetz, Manuel (2007): *Total Identity Made in Italy.* Total Identity.

Diemen, Stijn van (2005): *De waarde.* Total Identity.

Diemen, Stijn van (2011): *Be public. Be inspired. Be seen.* Total Identity.

Diemen, Stijn van (2012): *De traploze samenleving; Over de waarde van het onnutte.* Total Identity.

Glijn, Dennis and Diemen, Stijn van (2008): *Gedeelde drijfveren.* Total Identity.

Gioia, Dennis A. and Chittipeddi, Kumar (1991): 'Sensemaking and Sensegiving in Strategic Change Initiation.' *Strategic Management Journal*, Vol. 12, No. 6, pp. 433-448. John Wiley & Sons.

Heus, Edsco de and Berkhout, Dmitri (2009): *De corporate story als aanjager van identiteit van de financiële instelling.* Total Identity.

Houwen, Willemijn van der (2007): *Het psychologisch afstemmingsproces; Over het verwerven van een voorkeurspositie op de arbeidsmarkt.* Total Identity.

Kapferer, Jean-Noël (1995): *Les Marques, Capital de la Enterprise* (2ème ed.). Les Éditions d'Organisation.

Klein, Naomi (1999): *No Logo. Taking Aim at the Brand Bullies.* Knopf Canada / Picador.

Kroon, Elisabeth and Diemen, Stijn van (2008): *De transformatie; De zelfbewuste organisatie verkent haar toekomst.* Total Identity.

Lee, Bob van der and Diemen, Stijn van (2012): *Back to basics; Herwaardering van de maakindustrie in Nederland.* Total Identity.

Kim, W. Chan and Mauborgne, Renée (2005): *Blue Ocean Strategy; How to Create Uncontested Market Space and Make the Competition Irrelevant.* Harvard Business Review Press.

Kor, Rudy, Bos, Jo and Tak, Theo van der (2016): *Project Canvas; Samen naar de kern van je project.* Vakmedianet.

Mau, Bruce and the Institute without Boundaries (2004): *Massive Change.* Phaidon.

Morgan, Gareth (1992): *Beelden van organisatie [Images of Organisation].* Scriptum Books and Sage Publications.

OMA, Koolhaas, Rem and Mau, Bruce (1995): *Small, Medium, Large, Extra-Large.* 010 Publishers.

Osterwalder, Alexander and Pigneur, Yves (2010): *Business Model Generation; A Handbook for Visionaries, Game Changers, and Challengers.* John Wiley and Sons.

Papanek, Victor (1971/2019): *Design for the Real World* (3rd ed.). Thames & Hudson.

Pine, B. Joseph II and Gilmore, James H. (1999): *The Experience Economy.* Harvard Business School Press.

Porter, Michael (1980): *Competitive Strategy.* The Free Press.

Ries, Eric (2011): *The Lean Startup.* Crown Publising Group.

Rotmans, Jan (2012): *In het oog van de orkaan; Nederland in transitie.* Aeneas.

Schaminée, André (2018): *Designing With and within Public Organizations. Building Bridges Between Public Sector Innovators and Designers.* BIS Publishers.

Sennet, Richard (1998): *The Corrosion of Character.* Norton.

Sharpe, Bill (2020): *Three Horizons; The Patterning of Hope* (2nd ed.). International Futures Forum.

Sinek, Simon (2009): *Start with Why; How great leaders inspire everyone to take action.* Penguin.

Treacy, Michael and Wiersema, Fred (1995): *The Discipline of Market Leaders.* Perseus Publishing.

Verhaeghe, Paul (2012): *Identiteit.* Bezige Bij.

Stijn van Diemen (Laren (NL), 1963) studied modern Dutch literature and philosophy at the University of Amsterdam. He worked as an editor and designer for various cultural and government institutions and in 1988 founded the design agency and publishing house Plano, which he ran for ten years. He held various positions at Tel Design in The Hague, lived and worked for several years in Valencia and Madrid, and taught at the Amsterdam University of Applied Sciences. For almost fifteen years he worked for Total Identity (Total Design), as director of the The Hague office, later as group co-director. He then worked for a number of years as a strategy consultant at TwynstraGudde, before setting up his own strategy practice in 2020. He was a venture partner at Creative Capital Studio and currently also teaches at Utrecht University of Applied Sciences.

These environments have given him more than 30 years of experience in tackling strategic identity challenges in various sectors. With extensive consulting expertise in healthcare, education, government, ICT, digital platforms, industry associations and business services, both in the Netherlands and internationally, he has helped more than a hundred organisations, sectors and regions define and project their identity to build a successful future.

www.stijnvandiemen.com